MINNESOTA DRIVER'S PRACTICE TESTS

+ 360 DRIVING TEST QUESTIONS TO HELP YOU ACE YOUR DMV EXAM.

THE DRIVING SCHOOL

CONTENT

INTRODUCTION

First of all, thank you for choosing this book. As you work through it, you'll find a variety of questions to help you prepare for the DMV test. The questions are based on the information in the Driver's Manual of your state and each one is designed to help you better understand the material.

The best way to use the questions in this book is by practicing them. You can do that by following these steps:

- Take a diagnostic test so you may quickly detect gaps in your driving knowledge and obtain a rough estimate of how much you know about driving rules.
- Take the practice tests from beginning to end without stopping.
- After you have finished, review all of your incorrect answers and read the explanations provided, in the answer key, in the back of this book.
- Join the Facebook group and share questions or doubts with other students.

Remember, the more you practice, the better you'll perform on the real DMV exam.

In order to help you practice for your DMV test, each question has an answer and a corresponding explanation. In some cases, more than one answer might seem correct. In these cases, there will be explanations, after all of the possible responses, to help you understand why those answers are wrong and the other one is correct.

The MINNESOTA Driver's Handbook

The Minnesota Department of Motor Vehicles recommends that you study the official manual. Please read it at least once to get a feel of what you will need to know to pass your exam.

Scan the QR code or type the link in your browser to download it.

https://dps.mn.gov/divisions/dvs/forms-documents/Documents/Minnesota_Drivers_Manual.pdf

Cheat Sheets

Don't forget to download your Cheat Sheets, which will tremendously assist you in reviewing the top 100 questions on the DMV written test. Definitely worth reading before your exam. You will find them at the end of the book before the Answer Sheets.

We wish you the best of luck and encourage you to take our practice tests as many times as possible!

So don't wait any longer. Start studying today and you'll be ready to ace your DMV exam! Thanks again for choosing this book. We hope it helps you achieve your driving goals.

And don't forget to write a review of the book. We'd love to hear from you.

About us - The Driving School

We provide education services to people who want to learn how to drive. The company's mission is 'to provide safe and competent drivers for our streets and highways'. We achieve this mission by helping people pass their DMV written exams.

JOIN OUR FACEBOOK GROUP

Share your experience with other students and get answers to questions you might have! Scan the QR code below or type the link into your browser to join.

QR CODE

LINK TO THE GROUP

https://www.facebook.com/groups/953090518945188/

BONUSES

THE TOP 100 MOST FREQUENTLY ASKED QUESTIONS

Download the top 100 most frequently asked questions. We suggest you revise this document before your exam, so you can be fully prepared! Remember, the more you practice, the better you'll perform on the real DMV exam.

Type in your browser the following link or scan the QR Code

- https://dl.bookfunnel.com/lhf68zpx12

DIAGNOSTIC TEST

Are you just getting started with your study plan and don't know where to begin? With this DMV Diagnostic Test, you may quickly detect gaps in your driving knowledge and obtain a rough estimate of how much you know about driving rules.

Total Questions 15
Correct Answer to pass 12

Question 1 - Diagnostic Test

If you lost your driver's license for a reason other than DWI or criminal vehicular operation, you will be charged a reinstatement fee of _____.

- ☐ $20
- ☐ $50
- ☐ $100
- ☐ $30

Question 2 - Diagnostic Test

This sign denotes

- ☐ a roadblock in a construction zone
- ☐ an object marker on a roadway
- ☐ an interstate highway guide sign
- ☐ a caution sign in a construction zone

If you refuse to submit to chemical testing for alcohol or drug usage, your license will be suspended for at least

- ☐ 90 days
- ☐ 30 days
- ☐ 6 months
- ☐ 1 year

Question 4 - Diagnostic Test

This warning sign indicates

- ☐ a winding path
- ☐ there will be severe right and left twists ahead
- ☐ the road ahead curves to the right, then to the left
- ☐ the road ahead curves to the right

Question 5 - Diagnostic Test

In Minnesota, a yellow-painted curb indicates that drivers

- ☐ may not stop or park there
- ☐ may come to a halt until the route is clear to pass
- ☐ may only halt for the purpose of loading or unloading goods
- ☐ may simply stay there long enough to make a fast turn

Question 6 - Diagnostic Test

Above your lane, you notice a flashing yellow "X." What does it imply?

☐　　　Move into another lane as soon as it is safe to do so

☐　　　This lane is now closed

☐　　　This lane only allows for a left turn

☐　　　Proceed with extreme caution

Question 7 - Diagnostic Test

At a reduced conflict intersection, how do you make a left turn onto a divided highway?

☐　　　You can't do it. Continue to the next junction and perform a U-turn

☐　　　Turn left after entering the junction

☐　　　Continue straight before making a U-turn

☐　　　Make a right and then a U-turn

Question 8 - Diagnostic Test

You've arrived at an intersection. An emergency vehicle with flashing red lights and a siren or bell is on its way. So, what should you do now?

☐　　　Pull over to the left in the intersection

☐　　　Pull over to the right in the intersection

☐　　　Continue your journey at a faster pace

☐　　　Continue straight past the intersection and then pull over

Question 9 - Diagnostic Test

When you observe a reflective triangular sign on the back of a vehicle, you should

- ☐ come to a complete stop
- ☐ adjust your speed or get ready to switch lanes
- ☐ pass the vehicle by increasing your speed
- ☐ carry out any of the preceding actions

Question 10 - Diagnostic Test

If you use _____ simultaneously, you have a better chance of surviving a car accident.

- ☐ the lap belt and shoulder belt
- ☐ the shoulder belt, as well as the emergency lights
- ☐ the lap belt and a helmet
- ☐ none of the preceding

Question 11 - Diagnostic Test

Anyone who flees a police officer in a motor vehicle faces a maximum sentence of

- ☐ two years and one day
- ☐ five years and one day
- ☐ four years and one day
- ☐ three years and one day

Question 12 - Diagnostic Test

Towing a camper or trailer requires a following distance of at least _____ from other vehicles.

- ☐ 100 feet
- ☐ 200 feet
- ☐ 500 feet
- ☐ 600 feet

Question 13 - Diagnostic Test

You must _____ when passing another vehicle.

- ☐ return to the right side of the road before coming within 200 feet of an oncoming vehicle
- ☐ return to the right side of the road before coming within 100 feet of an oncoming vehicle
- ☐ return to the left side of the road before coming within 100 feet of an oncoming vehicle
- ☐ return to the left side of the road before coming within 200 feet of an oncoming vehicle

Question 14 - Diagnostic Test

You must _____ if you observe a steady yellow light as you approach an intersection.

- ☐ proceed with caution
- ☐ stop if possible
- ☐ continue to move at the same rate
- ☐ accelerate your pace

Most freeway entry ramps have _____ that allows you to raise your speed.

☐   a slow lane

☐   an access ramp

☐   an acceleration lane

☐   a deceleration lane

PRACTICE TEST 1

Get prepared for the DMV driving permit test exam by practicing with real questions that are very similar (often identical!) to those on the DMV test.

Total Questions: 40
Correct Answer to pass: 32

Question 1 - Practice Test 1

Yellow lines are used on one-way streets as

- ☐ lines on the right
- ☐ lines in the middle
- ☐ left-edge lines

Question 2 - Practice Test 1

What should you do to recover from hydroplaning?

- ☐ Hit the brakes
- ☐ Increase the amount of force you apply to the accelerator
- ☐ Firmly hit the brakes
- ☐ Take your foot off the gas pedal

Question 3 - Practice Test 1

When approaching and entering an acceleration lane, _____ to match the speed of vehicles in through lanes.

- ☐ Accelerate your pace
- ☐ Abruptly reduce your speed
- ☐ Gradually reduce your speed
- ☐ Alter your lane and accelerate

Question 4 - Practice Test 1

To get from a private road to a public road,

- ☐   you must first activate your four-way flashers
- ☐   perform a quick turn and enter the roadway, while blowing the horn
- ☐   you are not required to signal when entering the roadway
- ☐   you must come to a complete stop and yield to the vehicles on the road

Question 5 - Practice Test 1

In the event of a crash, your _____ protects your head and chest from colliding with the dashboard or windshield.

- ☐   head restraints
- ☐   lap belts
- ☐   shoulder belts
- ☐   steering wheel

Question 6 - Practice Test 1

Use your _____ when driving in fog, rain or snow.

- ☐   headlights with low-beams
- ☐   lights for parking
- ☐   four-way flashing lights
- ☐   high-intensity headlights

Question 7 - Practice Test 1

You may pass another vehicle on the right in which of the following situations?

    ☐   When the vehicle is preparing to make or is making a left turn

    ☐   When the vehicle is ready to make or is making a right turn

    ☐   When the vehicle is attempting to make a lane change

    ☐   None of the above options

Question 8 - Practice Test 1

In road accidents, 40% of fatalities are caused by a collision with the windshield, windshield frame or instrument panel. The majority of these deaths can be avoided by wearing:

    ☐   a windshield coating

    ☐   a waist belt

    ☐   safety goggles

    ☐   a shoulder belt

Question 9 - Practice Test 1

If you miss a freeway exit, you should

    ☐   stop and ask for assistance

    ☐   return to the exit by making a U-turn

    ☐   return to the exit by backing up

    ☐   proceed to the next exit

Question 10 - Practice Test 1

When two cars enter an uncontrolled intersection (one not controlled by signs or signals) from different highways at roughly the same time, the vehicle _____ has the right-of-way.

☐ on the right

☐ on the left

☐ signaling first

☐ with more passengers

Question 11 - Practice Test 1

If you notice an old person crossing a street, you should

☐ stop the person by blowing your horn

☐ yield the right-of-way by coming to a complete stop

☐ quickly cross the intersection by increasing your speed

☐ maintain your speed

Question 12 - Practice Test 1

If you see an emergency vehicle approaching with flashing red or blue lights and a siren, you must

☐ reduce your speed and take it slowly

☐ speed up to get out of the way

☐ pull over and come to a complete stop

☐ keep going at the same pace

Question 13 - Practice Test 1

If a bicycle on your right arrives at an uncontrolled intersection (one without signs or signals) around the same time as you, you should

- ☐ request that the bicyclist change lanes.

- ☐ proceed because you have the right-of-way.

- ☐ proceed slowly with the bicycle

- ☐ yield to the bicycle that arrives first

Question 14 - Practice Test 1

The danger zones around trucks and buses, where accidents are more prone to happen, are referred to as

- ☐ no-zones

- ☐ zones where no one is allowed to pass

- ☐ round-zones

- ☐ empty-zones

Question 15 - Practice Test 1

Tires that are unbalanced or have low tire pressures can cause

- ☐ reduced stopping distance

- ☐ tire wear that is accelerated

- ☐ increased fuel economy

- ☐ all of the abovementioned

Question 16 - Practice Test 1

As you reach and enter an acceleration lane:

- ☐ come to a complete stop, before attempting to merge into the motorway
- ☐ slowly merge into the motorway
- ☐ reduce your pace to match the speed of traffic in the through lanes
- ☐ increase your speed to keep up with the traffic in the through lanes

Question 17 - Practice Test 1

If you intend to turn past an intersection, you should

- ☐ not signal until you have reached the intersection
- ☐ provide a signal, just before you make the turn
- ☐ provide a signal, before entering the intersection
- ☐ not provide any turn signal

Question 18 - Practice Test 1

Except where prohibited, the three-point turn can be used to

- ☐ switch lanes.
- ☐ turn around on a narrow street
- ☐ pass another vehicle on a narrow road
- ☐ turn to the left

Question 19 - Practice Test 1

You should never share a lane with a motorcycle since

    ☐   the motorcycle requires the entire lane width

    ☐   motorcyclists are exempt from traffic laws

    ☐   you can be misguided by the motorcyclist

    ☐   motorcycles aren't equipped with turn signals

Question 20 - Practice Test 1

If your wheels stray onto the road's shoulder, you should:

    ☐   return to the road by increasing your speed

    ☐   swerve back onto the road, as soon as possible

    ☐   apply the brakes to bring the car to a complete stop

    ☐   slow down and keep on the shoulder

Question 21 - Practice Test 1

On a slick, rainy road, you're driving a vehicle without anti-lock brakes (ABS). What is the most effective approach to bring your vehicle to a stop?

    ☐   Remove your foot from the gas pedal

    ☐   Pump the brakes

    ☐   Firmly press the brake pedal

    ☐   Shift to the neutral position

Question 22 - Practice Test 1

Which is the correct hand signal to indicate a left turn?

☐ Upward-extended hand and arm

☐ Backwards-extended hand and arm

☐ Outwardly extended hand and arm

☐ hand and arm pointing downward

Question 23 - Practice Test 1

Looking ahead, to the sides and behind the car to foresee issues is an aspect of

☐ defensive driving

☐ distracted driving

☐ disciplined driving

☐ aggressive driving

Question 24 - Practice Test 1

Parking places for people with disabilities are indicated by _____ pavement markings.

☐ white

☐ red

☐ yellow

☐ blue

Question 25 - Practice Test 1

If you are stopped at a traffic light and another vehicle is approaching from behind at high speed,

☐   make a quick U-turn

☐   move your vehicle forward

☐   turn your vehicle to the right

☐   turn your vehicle to the left

Question 26 - Practice Test 1

If you have to park on the road, park your car

☐   as close as possible, to the center of the road

☐   as far away as possible, from the yellow line

☐   as far as possible, away from traffic

☐   as far as possible, away from the curb

Question 27 - Practice Test 1

The hand and arm bent at 90 degrees and pointing to the floor indicate the driver's intention to:

☐   make a turn to the left

☐   stop or slow down

☐   go straight ahead.

☐   make a turn to the right

Question 28 - Practice Test 1

Children under which age group should never be allowed to ride in the front seat of a car?

☐ 12 years old and under

☐ 14 years old and under

☐ 16 years old and under

☐ 13 years old and under

Question 29 - Practice Test 1

What should you do if you are the first person to arrive at the scene of a collision?

☐ Turn off the ignition of any vehicles involved in the collision

☐ Inform the local Police

☐ Remove your vehicle from the heavily traveled section of the road

☐ Carry out all of the preceding steps

Question 30 - Practice Test 1

Which of the following freeway claims are correct?

☐ Freeways are built to safely handle high-speed traffic

☐ Cross a solid line immediately after entering or before exiting, while using a freeway

☐ Deceleration lanes are available on most motorways to aid drivers in departing

☐ Smoothly enter a motorway by accelerating on the entry ramp to match the traffic pace

Question 31 - Practice Test 1

Which of the following claims about highway driving is correct?

- ☐ Faster cars must use the deceleration lane to join the highway

- ☐ The right lane provides the smoothest traffic flow, when there are three or more lanes, traveling in the same direction.

- ☐ The left lane should be used by slower vehicles, whereas the right lane should be used by quicker vehicles

- ☐ The right lane should be used by slower vehicles, while the left lane should be used by faster vehicles

Question 32 - Practice Test 1

Any vehicle's rear wheels will follow a _____, than its front wheels when it turns.

- ☐ shorter path

- ☐ longer path

- ☐ slower path

- ☐ faster path

Question 33 - Practice Test 1

Car and motorcycle collisions are more likely to happen in

- ☐ freeways

- ☐ roundabouts

- ☐ intersections

- ☐ one-way roads

Question 34 - Practice Test 1

A pair of white or longitudinal lines that indicate where pedestrians may walk, is known as

- ☐   lines of Suppression

- ☐   crosswalk lines

- ☐   pavement delineation

- ☐   lines for walking

Question 35 - Practice Test 1

In highway and street work zones, flag persons are operating

- ☐   to find out how much alcohol is in a driver's blood

- ☐   to safely stop, slow or direct vehicles through construction zones

- ☐   to slow vehicles down to the posted speed limit

- ☐   to notify the police and insurance companies about incidents

Question 36 - Practice Test 1

If a vehicle in front of you comes to a complete stop for a pedestrian at a crosswalk, you must

- ☐   change lanes rapidly and pass the vehicle

- ☐   not pass the car that has come to a complete halt

- ☐   reduce your speed and drive slowly past the vehicle

- ☐   proceed with caution after warning the pedestrian

Question 37 - Practice Test 1

When slowing down or coming to a complete stop, you must

- ☐ (a) make a hand signal to alert the driver in front of you.
- ☐ (b) use the brake-activated signal lights to warn the driver behind you.
- ☐ carry out either (a) or (b)
- ☐ carry out both (a) and (b)

Question 38 - Practice Test 1

What should you do to recover from a skid?

- ☐ Brake instantly and gently steer your vehicle in the opposite direction of where you want it to go
- ☐ Brake instantly and gently steer your vehicle in the direction you want it to go
- ☐ Take your foot off the throttle and slowly steer your vehicle in the direction you want it to go
- ☐ Take your foot off the accelerator and carefully steer your vehicle in the opposite direction of where you want it to travel

Question 39 - Practice Test 1

Which of the three types of intersections is correct?

- ☐ Diamond, blind and controlled
- ☐ Controlled, uncontrolled and blind
- ☐ Diamond, uncontrolled and controlled
- ☐ Cloverleaf, controlled and uncontrolled

All of the maneuvers listed below are correct while changing lanes, EXCEPT

☐ turning the steering wheel, when you turn your head to check for blind spots

☐ inspecting your rear-view and side-view mirrors

☐ removing your eyes from the ahead, for longer than a split second.

☐ looking over your shoulder in the direction you intend to move, whilst checking for blind spots

PRACTICE TEST 2

Get prepared for the DMV driving permit test exam by practicing with real questions that are very similar (often identical!) to those on the DMV test.

Total Questions: 40
Correct Answer to pass: 32

Question 1 - Practice Test 2

On a roadway, the left lane should be used for

- ☐ departing
- ☐ crossing over.
- ☐ passing
- ☐ backing up

Question 2 - Practice Test 2

Which of the following types of signs inform you of potential dangers ahead?

- ☐ Informational signs
- ☐ Regulatory signs
- ☐ Warning signs
- ☐ Guide signs

Question 3 - Practice Test 2

You can turn your vehicle around by making _____ when there is no traffic on either side of the road.

☐　　a two-point turn

☐　　a four-point turn

☐　　a single-point turn

☐　　a three-point turn

Question 4 - Practice Test 2

While passing a large vehicle, such as a truck, do not merge back in front of it until you can view its

☐　　headlights in your left side mirror

☐　　headlights in your rear-view mirror

☐　　headlights in your right side mirror

☐　　driver in your left side mirror

Question 5 - Practice Test 2

What does this signal mean?

☐　　You should stop

☐　　If the intersection is clear, you may proceed

☐　　You need to slow down

☐　　You may accelerate

Question 6 - Practice Test 2

It is best to stay _____ of your lane.

☐   in any part

☐   on the right side

☐   on the left side

☐   in the middle

Question 7 - Practice Test 2

Use high-beam headlights at night

☐   in the construction zones

☐   when there may be people on the road

☐   on unfamiliar roads

☐   in all of the preceding circumstances

Question 8 - Practice Test 2

The section of the expressway beyond the solid white line is designated for

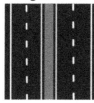

☐   emergency use only

☐   parking only

☐   stopping only

☐   U-turns only

Question 9 - Practice Test 2

If there is a solid white line adjacent to your lane, you should

- ☐ not remain in your lane
- ☐ stay in your lane
- ☐ stop at the line
- ☐ make a right turn

Question 10 - Practice Test 2

Use the _____ when driving in fog, rain, or snow.

- ☐ hazard lights
- ☐ high-beam headlights
- ☐ low-beam headlights
- ☐ parking lights

Question 11 - Practice Test 2

To pass another vehicle, keep a safe distance and do not _____ until the path is clear.

- ☐ re-enter the passing lane
- ☐ accelerate your pace
- ☐ straighten up
- ☐ re-enter your original lane

Question 12 - Practice Test 2

What does the abbreviation CDS stand for?

- ☐   Controlled Drugs and Substances
- ☐   Controlled Dangerous Substance
- ☐   Complex Drugs Substances
- ☐   None of the preceding

Question 13 - Practice Test 2

Which of the following statements regarding safety belt is baseless?

- ☐   They should be worn low and snug on the hips, with a tight cross-over across the shoulder
- ☐   You will be trapped after an accident if you wear a safety belt
- ☐   They slow your body down with your car
- ☐   They prevent you from being thrown from the vehicle

Question 14 - Practice Test 2

A car's stopping distance is equal to

- ☐   the sum of its reaction distance and braking distance
- ☐   its braking distance
- ☐   the sum of its reaction distance and following distance
- ☐   the sum of its braking distance and following distance

Question 15 - Practice Test 2

Rumble strips employ vibration and sound to warn drowsy or inattentive drivers that they are

- ☐ approaching a highway
- ☐ coming up to a stop sign or signal
- ☐ approaching a parking lot or a recreational area
- ☐ getting close to a school zone

Question 16 - Practice Test 2

_____ are mobile gadgets that provide drivers with advance notice of construction zones or other unusual conditions.

- ☐ Drums
- ☐ Barricades
- ☐ Flashing arrow panels
- ☐ Vertical panels

Question 17 - Practice Test 2

If your car is hit from the side, your body will be thrown towards

- ☐ the side that has been struck
- ☐ the front
- ☐ the back
- ☐ the side opposing the one that is struck

Question 18 - Practice Test 2

If you are exiting a high-speed, two-lane highway, _____ if there is traffic behind you.

☐   reduce your speed as soon as possible

☐   brake hard and keep the steering steady

☐   try not to slow down suddenly

☐   accelerate

Question 19 - Practice Test 2

If an animal runs in front of your car, you must

☐   drive around the animal as swiftly as possible

☐   proceed after sounding your horn

☐   keep your focus on maintaining control of your vehicle

☐   break as hard as you possibly can

Question 20 - Practice Test 2

Locked wheel skids are frequently the result of

☐   the driving wheels losing grip on the road

☐   excessive braking at high speeds

☐   simultaneously depressing the throttle and braking pedals

☐   the ignition turned to the lock position

Question 21 - Practice Test 2

What should you do if some of your visitors wish to drive home after drinking heavily?

☐ Instruct them to drive slowly

☐ Tell them to wait 30 minutes before driving

☐ Invite them to stay overnight

☐ Before they go, offer them coffee

Question 22 - Practice Test 2

If your rear wheels begin to skid, what should you do?

☐ Turn your steering wheel to the right

☐ Turn your steering wheel in the opposite direction of the skid

☐ Turn your steering wheel in the skid's direction

☐ Turn the steering wheel to the left

Question 23 - Practice Test 2

While making a left turn at a controlled intersection, you must yield to

☐ oncoming traffic

☐ vehicles on the right

☐ vehicles following you

☐ vehicles making a right turn

The white line placed across each approach lane at this crossroads indicates

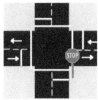

☐   the point before which your vehicle must come to a complete stop

☐   the point beyond which no right turn is permitted

☐   the point at which the route becomes impassable

☐   the speed limit beyond which you shall not exceed

Question 25 - Practice Test 2

Turning left from a two-way street onto a one-way street requires you to

☐   begin the turn with your right wheel as close to the yellow dividing line as possible

☐   begin the turn with your left wheel as close to the yellow dividing line as possible

☐   swing wide to the right before turning

☐   carry out any of the preceding actions

Question 26 - Practice Test 2

When driving in city traffic, you should try to look at least

☐   two blocks ahead

☐   three blocks ahead

☐   four blocks ahead

☐   a block ahead

Question 27 - Practice Test 2

You must check for traffic _____, before changing lanes.

- ☐ in front of your vehicle
- ☐ to the side of your vehicle
- ☐ both behind and to the side of your vehicle
- ☐ neither behind nor to the side of your vehicle

Question 28 - Practice Test 2

You should not _____ if your brakes fail while you are on the road.

- ☐ rub the tires up against a curb
- ☐ shift down into a lower gear
- ☐ stop by hitting with a solid object head-on
- ☐ press down on the brake pedal

Question 29 - Practice Test 2

The shape of this symbol forewarns of

- ☐ a no-passing zone ahead
- ☐ no-zone zone ahead
- ☐ a two-way street ahead
- ☐ a merging traffic

Question 30 - Practice Test 2

A motorcycle or moped

- ☐ is more difficult to see than other vehicles
- ☐ cannot be hidden in your blind spot
- ☐ is more visible than other vehicles
- ☐ cannot be easily missed

Question 31 - Practice Test 2

When you want to change lanes, look over your shoulder in the direction you want to go to make sure there are no other vehicles in

- ☐ no-passing zones
- ☐ shoulder zones
- ☐ blind spots
- ☐ free zones

Question 32 - Practice Test 2

If you intend to turn after passing beyond an intersection, you should

- ☐ not give any turn signal
- ☐ signal before you pass through the intersection
- ☐ signal just after you pass through the intersection
- ☐ signal just before you make the turn

Question 33 - Practice Test 2

You should be able to stop safely in wet, icy, or snowy conditions by

- ☐ frequently changing lanes
- ☐ making use of high-beam headlights
- ☐ accelerating your pace
- ☐ extending your following distance

Question 34 - Practice Test 2

It is recommended to _____ for better traction when driving in icy conditions.

- ☐ decrease your speed by 5 mph
- ☐ use chains
- ☐ accelerate
- ☐ drive on the road's shoulder

Question 35 - Practice Test 2

You should not _____ if a tire blows out.

- ☐ move to the road's shoulder as soon as possible
- ☐ apply the brakes lightly if necessary and safe to do so
- ☐ firmly grab the steering wheel
- ☐ take your foot off the gas pedal

Question 36 - Practice Test 2

You're at an intersection, and you're taking a left on a green arrow signal. The arrow signal then turns yellow. So, what should you do now?

- ☐ Make a U-turn
- ☐ Complete your turn
- ☐ Wait for a green arrow to stop
- ☐ You should slow down

Question 37 - Practice Test 2

Avoid _____ crossing railroad tracks.

- ☐ making use of your high-beam headlights
- ☐ stopping or shifting gears
- ☐ Make use of your low-beam headlights
- ☐ using the brakes

Question 38 - Practice Test 2

Suppose your vehicle's turn signals fail, use

- ☐ emergency signals
- ☐ parking signals
- ☐ stop signals
- ☐ hand signals

Question 39 - Practice Test 2

You must not _____ when making a U-turn.

☐   give a turn signal

☐   make it on a road curve or on a slope with insufficient visibility

☐   allow oncoming traffic the right-of-way

☐   allow pedestrians the right-of-way

Question 40 - Practice Test 2

Some streets and highways have diagonal yellow stripes that indicate

☐   (a) the road is becoming narrow

☐   (b) there is an obstruction on the roadway

☐   either (a) or (b)

☐   neither (a) nor (b)

ROAD SIGNS

In the United States, road signs are increasingly using symbols rather than words to convey their message. Symbols allow for immediate communication with road users, overcoming language barriers and are fast becoming the industry standard for traffic control equipment around the world.

Every car driver should be familiar with the symbols on traffic signs to ensure the safety and efficiency of our transportation systems.

We've got you covered with more than 150 questions on Road Signs.

Total Questions: 150
Correct Answer to pass: 120

Question 1 - Road Signs

This symbol indicates

- ☐   a railroad crossing
- ☐   work on the road
- ☐   a left turn
- ☐   road maintenance

Question 2 - Road Signs

What is the significance of this flashing arrow panel?

◻   The lane ahead has been closed

◻   The lane ahead of you is open for traffic

◻   Flaggers (people who wave flags) are in front

◻   The left lane curves ahead

Question 3 - Road Signs

This symbol indicates

◻   the distance between the current exit and the next

◻   an interstate highway number

◻   a code of exit

◻   the speed limit on interstate highways

Question 4 - Road Signs

This symbol indicates

☐ vehicles on the left must turn left, while vehicles on the right must continue straight

☐ vehicles on the left must make a left turn and vehicles on the right must make a right turn

☐ vehicles on the left must turn left, while vehicles on the right may either continue straight or turn left

☐ vehicles on the left must turn left, while those on the right must merge with the right lane

Question 5 - Road Signs

This diagram depicts

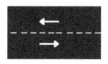

☐ a crossroads that lies ahead

☐ a two-way road

☐ a one-way road

☐ crossing traffic is ahead.

Question 6 - Road Signs

What does this sign mean?

- ☐   A divided highway begins ahead of you
- ☐   There will be one-way traffic ahead
- ☐   The divided highway comes to an end ahead
- ☐   Traffic is congealing ahead

Question 7 - Road Signs

What does this sign mean?

- ☐   When the green arrow is illuminated, left turns are permitted
- ☐   When the steady green signal is illuminated and there are no oncoming vehicles, left turns are permitted
- ☐   When the green arrow flashes, no left turns are permitted
- ☐   Left turns are only permitted when the steady green signal is not illuminated

Question 8 - Road Signs

What does this sign mean?

- ☐ Traffic in the right lane must merge to the right, while traffic in the second lane must either go straight or merge to the right
- ☐ The traffic in the right lane must continue straight, while the traffic in the second lane must turn right
- ☐ Traffic in the right lane must turn right, while traffic in the second lane must either stay straight or turn left
- ☐ Traffic in the right lane must turn right, while traffic in the second lane must either stay straight or turn right

Question 9 - Road Signs

What exactly does this sign mean?

- ☐ There is disabled parking ahead
- ☐ There is a disabled crossing ahead
- ☐ A hospital is on the way
- ☐ There is a pedestrian crosswalk ahead

Question 10 - Road Signs

This warning sign informs drivers that

- ☐ there is a single-use path crossing ahead

- ☐ there is a school zone ahead

- ☐ bicyclists must be allowed to use the lane

- ☐ there is a multi-use path crossing ahead

Question 11 - Road Signs

What exactly does this sign mean?

- ☐ There is a tunnel ahead

- ☐ There is a railroad crossing ahead

- ☐ A work zone awaits

- ☐ A crossroads awaits

Question 12 - Road Signs

What does this image represent?

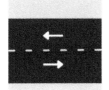

  ☐   When the road ahead is clear, passing on the left is permitted

  ☐   Passing on the left is not permitted

  ☐   Passing is prohibited in both directions

  ☐   Passing is only permitted during the day

Question 13 - Road Signs

What exactly does this road sign mean?

  ☐   A construction zone is ahead

  ☐   A parking area is ahead

  ☐   The forest zone is ahead

  ☐   There's a rest stop ahead

Question 14 - Road Signs

What does this figure represent?

○   A child care center is on the way

○   There is a T-intersection ahead

○   A playground lies ahead

○   There is a school zone ahead.

Question 15 - Road Signs

This symbol is

○   a service sign

○   a route-marking sign

○   a regulatory indication

○   a cautionary note

Question 16 - Road Signs

What does this sign mean?

☐   A side street near a railroad crossing

☐   A slender bridge

☐   A truck service center

☐   A pedestrian overpass

Question 17 - Road Signs

This symbol indicates

☐   a hospital area

☐   wheelchair accessibility is available

☐   a parking area for the handicapped

☐   a crosswalk for pedestrians

Question 18 - Road Signs

This orange triangular reflective sign represents

☐   a rapidly moving vehicle

☐   a vehicle transporting dangerous materials

☐   a slow-moving vehicle

☐   a large truck

Question 19 - Road Signs

Which of these signs points you in the direction of a hospital?

A   B   C   D

☐   D

☐   B

☐   A

☐   C

Question 20 - Road Signs

What does this sign mean?

☐   Vehicles are merging ahead, do not accelerate to 45 mph

☐   Drive at a 45-mph speed

☐   A speed zone is ahead, prepare to slow down to 45 mph

☐   Construction ahead, slow down to 45 mph.

Question 21 - Road Signs

Typically, a vertical, rectangular traffic sign provides

☐   guidelines to the driver

☐   directions to the driver to come to a halt

☐   a road number

☐   a warning about the road's condition

Question 22 - Road Signs

This symbol indicates

  ☐   a lane for turning right

  ☐   a diversion

  ☐   the road ahead curves to the left.

  ☐   a lane for turning left

Question 23 - Road Signs

This symbol indicates that

  ☐   bicyclists should only ride in the lane designated by the sign

  ☐   a bikeway crosses the road ahead

  ☐   bicyclists are not permitted to use this lane

  ☐   there is a no-passing zone for bicyclists ahead

Question 24 - Road Signs

If you see this sign while driving in the left lane, what should you do?

- ☐ Continue straight
- ☐ Merge into the right lane
- ☐ Take a left
- ☐ Take a right

Question 25 - Road Signs

This is a warning sign denoting

- ☐ there will be sharp right and left turns ahead
- ☐ the road ahead takes a right turn
- ☐ a winding path
- ☐ the road ahead bends to the right, then to the left

Question 26 - Road Signs

What does this signal mean at an intersection?

- ☐ Pedestrians are not permitted to enter the crosswalk
- ☐ Drivers must slow down and exercise caution
- ☐ Pedestrians who are already in the crosswalk may complete their crossing
- ☐ Pedestrians are permitted to enter the crosswalk

Question 27 - Road Signs

This symbol indicates

- ☐ there is a hospital ahead
- ☐ there is a rest stop ahead
- ☐ a high school awaits
- ☐ there is a handicapped service area ahead

Question 28 - Road Signs

What does this image represent?

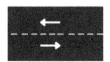

- ○   Under no circumstances, are vehicles permitted to cross the broken yellow line

- ○   Vehicles are not permitted to pass or turn across the broken yellow line

- ○   Vehicles are only permitted to cross the broken yellow line if it is safe to do so

- ○   If it is safe to do so, vehicles may cross the broken yellow line, to pass or turn

Question 29 - Road Signs

This symbol indicates

- ○   That Exit number 117 is up ahead

- ○   the next available exit is 117 miles away

- ○   to get onto Route 117, take this exit.

- ○   none of the aforementioned.

Question 30 - Road Signs

This sign indicates the location of

   ☐   a gas station

   ☐   a communication service

   ☐   a place to rest

   ☐   a camping area

Question 31 - Road Signs

What does this sign mean?

   ☐   The divided highway comes to an end ahead

   ☐   A divided highway begins ahead of you

   ☐   There's an underpass ahead of you

   ☐   The right lane is closed ahead

Question 32 - Road Signs

These highway signs are known as

○   dynamic message signs

○   route marker signs

○   crossroads indicators

○   work zone markers

Question 33 - Road Signs

If you see this sign, it means you are

○   moving in the wrong lane

○   driving in the wrong direction

○   in the city

○   on the highway

Question 34 - Road Signs

What exactly does this sign mean?

- ☐   At night, take Route 45

- ☐   The top speed is 45 miles per hour.

- ☐   The minimum speed limit is 45 miles per hour

- ☐   At night, the maximum speed limit is 45 mph

Question 35 - Road Signs

What exactly does this sign mean?

- ☐   There is a possibility that emergency vehicles will enter the roadway

- ☐   Trucks transporting dangerous materials may enter the road

- ☐   Heavy vehicles may enter the road

- ☐   Farm vehicles have the potential to enter the roadway

Question 36 - Road Signs

What should you do if you come across this sign at an intersection?

- ☐ Do not go any further
- ☐ Continue to the right
- ☐ Allow oncoming traffic to pass
- ☐ Before turning right or left, yield the right-of-way or come to a complete stop

Question 37 - Road Signs

This sign and the pavement markings permits

- ☐ vehicles approaching from either direction to make a right turn
- ☐ vehicles from either direction are permitted to pass
- ☐ vehicles approaching from either direction to make a left turn
- ☐ none of the aforementioned.

Question 38 - Road Signs

What exactly does this sign mean?

☐   At the sign, all vehicles must make a U-turn

☐   U-turns are not permitted for trucks

☐   Vehicles are not permitted to make a U-turn at the sign

☐   It denotes none of the preceding

Question 39 - Road Signs

What exactly does this sign mean?

☐   A side road is ahead, keep an eye out for vehicles entering the road

☐   There will be a T-intersection ahead, yield to cross traffic

☐   There will be a four-way stop ahead, prepare to yield

☐   A tourist information center is ahead, make a stop if necessary

Question 40 - Road Signs

What does this sign mean?

☐   There's a speed limit ahead

☐   On-ramp speed restriction

☐   Speed advisory at the roundabout

☐   Exit speed restriction

Question 41 - Road Signs

What exactly does this sign mean?

☐   Only right turns are permitted

☐   Traffic must merge to the right

☐   Traffic must merge to the left

☐   Only left turns are permitted

Question 42 - Road Signs

What exactly does this sign mean?

- ☐ You must not take a right turn
- ☐ You must not turn left
- ☐ This section of the road is currently closed
- ☐ Do not combine

Question 43 - Road Signs

What exactly does this sign mean?

- ☐ A hospital is on the way
- ☐ There is a telephone service available ahead
- ☐ There will be a gas station ahead
- ☐ There will be a rest stop ahead

Question 44 - Road Signs

What exactly does this sign mean?

- ☐ You're about to approach a left turn
- ☐ You're about to approach a right turn
- ☐ A sharp U-turn is on the way
- ☐ A sharp left turn awaits

Question 45 - Road Signs

What should you do if you see this road sign?

- ☐ Exit the highway at a minimum speed of 30 miles per hour
- ☐ Exit the highway at a speed of 30 miles per hour or less
- ☐ Pass the vehicle in front of you by increasing your speed to 30 mph
- ☐ With a top speed of 60 mph, exit the highway

Question 46 - Road Signs

This image's pavement markings indicate that

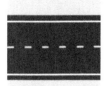

☐   it is not permitted to pass

☐   it is permissible to pass

☐   drivers are required to take a detour

☐   drivers must make a turn

Question 47 - Road Signs

What is the nature of this sign?

☐   A sign saying 'Do Not Enter'

☐   A yield sign

☐   A stop sign

☐   A one-way street sign

Question 48 - Road Signs

What does this traffic sign mean?

- ☐ Passing a vehicle on the left is not permitted
- ☐ Only left turns are permitted
- ☐ In these directions, passing is permitted
- ☐ Only move in the directions indicated

Question 49 - Road Signs

What exactly does this sign mean?

- ☐ A hospital is near
- ☐ Approaching a four-way intersection
- ☐ There's a side road ahead
- ☐ There is a railroad crossing ahead

Question 50 - Road Signs

What exactly does this sign mean?

- ☐ Large trucks are not permitted on this road
- ☐ Trucks are not permitted to park here
- ☐ On this road, only large trucks are permitted
- ☐ On this road, only high-occupancy vehicles (HOVs) are permitted

Question 51 - Road Signs

This symbol indicates

- ☐ a railroad crossing with low ground clearance
- ☐ a railroad crossing that is closed
- ☐ a railroad crossing that is being repaired
- ☐ a byway near a railroad crossing

Question 52 - Road Signs

What does this image represent?

☐   A shattered white line that forbids passing

☐   A broken white line that permits passing

☐   An accident occurred as a result of a shorter following
     distance.

☐   A vehicle making a U-turn

Question 53 - Road Signs

This is an octagonal (eight-sided) figure which means

☐   a yield symbol

☐   a sign that says 'Do Not Enter'

☐   a stop sign

☐   a construction sign on a road

This orange sign can be found at

☐   crossings of railroads

☐   intersections that are uncontrolled

☐   zones around schools

☐   work zones

Question 55 - Road Signs

This symbol can be used to

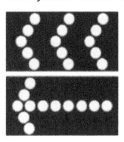

☐   direct drivers into specific traffic lanes

☐   direct drivers to perform a U-turn

☐   warn drivers that there is a one-way street ahead

☐   make drivers aware of the presence of a school zone

Question 56 - Road Signs

This sign informs the driver that the road is a

- ☐ a winding road
- ☐ a double curve
- ☐ the road is slick.
- ☐ a two-way street

Question 57 - Road Signs

This sign expresses concern that

- ☐ a winding road awaits, drivers should follow the signs
- ☐ there is a gravel road ahead with sharp curves, drivers must proceed with caution
- ☐ when the road is wet, it becomes slick and drivers must proceed cautiously
- ☐ there is a sharp curve near a hill, vehicles must proceed cautiously

Question 58 - Road Signs

This symbol is a

- ☐   sign that says 'Right Lane Ends'

- ☐   sign for a freeway interchange

- ☐   sharp turn on a highway

- ☐   beginning of a Divided Highway sign

Question 59 - Road Signs

This diamond-shaped symbol denotes

- ☐   there is a median ahead, the road width is 13 feet 6 inches

- ☐   there is a bridge ahead, the road width is 13 feet 6 inches

- ☐   there is an overpass ahead with a clearance of 13 feet 6 inches from the roadway surface to the overpass

- ☐   there is a parking area ahead, the road width is 13 feet 6 inches

Question 60 - Road Signs

What exactly does this sign mean?

☐   You are not permitted to park on either side of the sign

☐   You can park on the left side of the sign at night

☐   Parking is available to the left of the sign

☐   You are not permitted to park to the left of the sign

Question 61 - Road Signs

What does this sign mean?

☐   A deer is crossing ahead

☐   A cattle crossing is ahead

☐   The forest zone is ahead

☐   There is a zoo ahead

Question 62 - Road Signs

What does this sign mean?

○   At any time, the maximum permissible speed in a school zone

○   At any time, the minimum permissible speed in a school zone

○   When there are children present in a school zone, this is the maximum permissible speed

○   When there are children present in a school zone, this is the minimum permissible speed

Question 63 - Road Signs

This service sign specifies that

○   there is parking available

○   there is lodging available

○   there is a hospital service available

○   there is a service area available

What is the significance of this regulatory sign?

☐ During the times specified, the indicated lane is for high-occupancy vehicles

☐ High-occupancy vehicles are not permitted at certain times

☐ During the specified times, no cars or buses are permitted

☐ The designated lane is for large trucks

Question 65 - Road Signs

A stop sign accompanied by this sign at an intersection indicates that

☐ you must come to a complete stop for four seconds.

☐ there are four traffic lanes.

☐ vehicles approaching from all four directions must yield

☐ vehicles approaching the intersection from all four directions must come to a complete stop

Question 66 - Road Signs

What exactly does this sign mean?

- ☐   The road ahead is closed
- ☐   This road comes to an end at a T-intersection
- ☐   A narrow bridge's rails are ahead
- ☐   There will be a Y-intersection ahead

Question 67 - Road Signs

This symbol indicates

- ☐   to enter Route 47 north, make a right turn
- ☐   Route 47 north has one-way traffic
- ☐   the start of Route 47 north
- ☐   Route 47 has come to an end

Question 68 - Road Signs

What exactly does this sign mean?

☐ There will be an RC flying zone ahead

☐ You're getting close to an airport

☐ In this zone, planes fly at low altitudes

☐ This is the direction in which planes fly

Question 69 - Road Signs

This highway sign indicates

☐ a forthcoming side road

☐ a forthcoming three-way stop

☐ there is a railroad crossing ahead

☐ a side road with restricted access

Question 70 - Road Signs

This symbol indicates

☐　　a transition

☐　　a sharp turn

☐　　an emergency halt

☐　　a diversion

Question 71 - Road Signs

This publicly displayed sign is

☐　　on hills, there is a speed limit sign

☐　　at roundabouts, there is a speed limit sign

☐　　a sign indicating an interstate route

☐　　a speed limit sign on expressways

Question 72 - Road Signs

Which of the following signs denotes a school zone?

A B C D

- ☐   D
- ☐   C
- ☐   B
- ☐   A

Question 73 - Road Signs

What does this stop sign mean?

- ☐   In 1,000 feet, there will be construction
- ☐   After 1,000 feet, turning right is prohibited
- ☐   An alternate route is available 1,000 feet ahead
- ☐   There will be a parking zone ahead

Question 74 - Road Signs

This symbol indicates

☐   a median is on the way.

☐   there is a bump in the road ahead

☐   a steep incline awaits

☐   the road ahead has an incline

Question 75 - Road Signs

What does this signal indicate?

☐   You must not take a right turn

☐   You must not walk

☐   Do not combine

☐   Do not proceed

Question 76 - Road Signs

These pavement markings denote

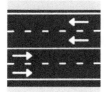

☐ except when turning left, vehicles must not cross the solid yellow line

☐ except to pass, vehicles must not cross the solid yellow line

☐ under no circumstances should a vehicle cross the broken white lines

☐ none of the aforementioned

Question 77 - Road Signs

What exactly does this sign mean?

☐ Stop ahead

☐ A pedestrian zone ahead

☐ Turn right ahead

☐ Flag person ahead

Question 78 - Road Signs

This symbol indicates

   ☐   traffic is merging ahead

   ☐   the terminus of a divided highway

   ☐   a two-way street

   ☐   a narrow street

Question 79 - Road Signs

What exactly does this sign mean?

   ☐   A narrow bridge lies ahead

   ☐   There's an acceleration lane ahead

   ☐   Hidden traffic is ahead

   ☐   The road ahead is narrow

Question 80 - Road Signs

What does this sign mean?

☐   The left lane comes to an end ahead

☐   The right lane comes to an end ahead

☐   A one-way street awaits

☐   A narrow bridge awaits you ahead

Question 81 - Road Signs

A flashing red light indicates that you must_____ before proceeding.

☐   slow down

☐   turn and drive carefully

☐   stop

☐   not stop

Question 82 - Road Signs

This figure's single broken (dashed) white line denotes

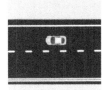

- ☐ traffic flowing in opposing directions

- ☐ all traffic is moving in the same direction

- ☐ the road's shoulder

- ☐ a section of a road where passing is prohibited

Question 83 - Road Signs

What does this sign mean?

- ☐ A school area

- ☐ A flagger in a construction zone

- ☐ A road crew at work

- ☐ At an intersection, there is a pedestrian crosswalk

Question 84 - Road Signs

What is the significance of this warning sign?

- [ ] There will be a stop sign ahead
- [ ] A yield sign is on the way
- [ ] Slow-moving vehicles should not follow the directions
- [ ] Slow-moving vehicles should follow directions

Question 85 - Road Signs

This sign warns drivers about

- [ ] a bus stop for students
- [ ] a play area for children
- [ ] a school zone
- [ ] the pedestrian crosswalks at an intersection

Question 86 - Road Signs

What is the significance of this regulatory sign?

    ☐   Do not merge to the left

    ☐   You must take a right

    ☐   Right turns are not permitted

    ☐   Turning left is not permitted

Question 87 - Road Signs

The number depicted in this sign stands for

    ☐   a sign indicating a U.S. route

    ☐   an exit number

    ☐   the distance from the exit

    ☐   the exit ramp's speed limit

Question 88 - Road Signs

This sign alerts drivers that they

☐   must not leave the pavement

☐   should extend their following distance to 6 seconds

☐   should move quickly onto the shoulder

☐   must move onto the shoulder at a slower pace

Question 89 - Road Signs

What exactly does this sign mean?

☐   Keep to the left of the divider

☐   You're getting close to a divided highway

☐   You'll have to take a detour

☐   Keep to the right of the divider

Question 90 - Road Signs

What exactly does this sign mean?

☐ You are not permitted to drive on the railroad tracks

☐ A railroad crossing is ahead

☐ You have permission to drive on the railroad tracks

☐ You must come to a halt at the railroad tracks

Question 91 - Road Signs

What exactly does this sign mean?

☐ Pedestrians ahead, no vehicle access

☐ Slow down and exercise extreme caution

☐ Stop to allow for pedestrians

☐ Pedestrians are not permitted to cross

Which of the following signs indicates two-way traffic?

A   B   C   D

- ☐   C
- ☐   D
- ☐   B
- ☐   A

Question 93 - Road Signs

You may travel in the lane indicated by this sign.

- ☐   Only if you're on a bicycle
- ☐   If you're passing the car in front of you
- ☐   If you're on a motorcycle
- ☐   If you're transporting two or more people

Question 94 - Road Signs

What exactly does this sign mean?

☐   There is a Y-intersection ahead

☐   There's a side road ahead

☐   A youth hostel awaits

☐   There is a yield sign ahead

Question 95 - Road Signs

This symbol denotes

☐   the speed limit on the interstate highway

☐   the distance between the current exit and the next

☐   the exit code

☐   the interstate highway number

Question 96 - Road Signs

This sign indicates that the parking spaces are for

☐ elderly people

☐ riders

☐ people with disabilities

☐ patients

Question 97 - Road Signs

What exactly does this road sign mean?

☐ Farmhouse on the way

☐ A cattle crossing is ahead

☐ Following is a veterinary hospital

☐ Next stop, the zoo

Question 98 - Road Signs

What exactly does this sign mean?

   ☐   It is not permitted to stop or stand

   ☐   A tunnel is ahead of you

   ☐   Hitchhiking is not permitted

   ☐   You're getting close to a school zone

Question 99 - Road Signs

This symbol denotes

   ☐   the maximum number of vehicles permitted to park

   ☐   the top speed limit on a road

   ☐   a checkpoint

   ☐   a sign indicating a U.S. route marker

Question 100 - Road Signs

What does this figure represent?

☐   A flag person is ahead, proceed with caution

☐   A crew is on the job, so vehicles must slow down

☐   There is a pedestrian crossing ahead, vehicles must yield

☐   A school crossing is ahead, vehicles must come to a complete stop

Question 101 - Road Signs

What does this sign mean?

☐   A high-occupancy vehicle no-passing zone

☐   All vehicles are prohibited from passing through this area

☐   Trucks are not permitted to pass through this area

☐   A school bus no-passing zone

What does this sign mean?

   ☐   Bicyclists are not permitted to be passed by vehicles

   ☐   This road is only for bicyclists to use

   ☐   Bicyclists are not permitted to use this road

   ☐   Bicyclists are not permitted to pass through this area

Question 103 - Road Signs

This symbol is

   ☐   a warning sign in a construction zone

   ☐   a barricade in a construction zone

   ☐   an interstate highway guide sign

   ☐   an object marker on a roadway

Question 104 - Road Signs

It is now 9:30 a.m. Is it legal for you to park next to this sign?

☐   Yes, but only for a period of five minutes

☐   No

☐   Yes, but only if you have a special permit

☐   Yes

Question 105 - Road Signs

What does this symbol mean?

☐   The road shoulder is significantly lower than the road surface

☐   The road is slick and flooded

☐   This is a back road

☐   The road is strewn with gravel

Question 106 - Road Signs

This sign could be displayed

- ☐   close to hospitals
- ☐   in no-parking zones
- ☐   at intersections
- ☐   in construction zones

Question 107 - Road Signs

What exactly does this sign mean?

- ☐   The railroad ahead of you is closed for maintenance
- ☐   There will be a railroad crossing ahead
- ☐   A new railroad is being built
- ☐   The road ahead is closed for maintenance

Question 108 - Road Signs

When you come across this sign, you're driving at 65 mph. What does it imply?

☐   You'll need to slow down ahead

☐   You can keep going at your current rate

☐   You'll have to pick up the pace

☐   You're getting close to a school zone

Question 109 - Road Signs

If you see this sign, you must drive at a speed of at least

☐   At least 40 miles per hour

☐   At least 50 miles per hour

☐   No faster than 50 mph

☐   No faster than 40 mph

Question 110 - Road Signs

This steady red X signal above a highway lane indicates that

☐   you are not permitted to drive in this lane

☐   you must only drive in this lane

☐   you are welcome to use this lane

☐   you must come to a complete stop in this lane

Question 111 - Road Signs

What exactly does this sign mean?

☐   Trucks are not permitted to enter or cross this road

☐   Hazardous materials-carrying vehicles may enter or cross this roadway

☐   This roadway may be entered or crossed by high-occupancy vehicles

☐   Trucks may enter or exit this road

Question 112 - Road Signs

What exactly does this sign mean?

☐   Drivers may need to shift into a lower gear due to the steep descent ahead

☐   A narrow road near a hill, drivers must proceed cautiously

☐   There will be a bump ahead, drivers must maintain a consistent speed

☐   A freeway acceleration ramp, drivers must merge with freeway traffic

Question 113 - Road Signs

This symbol indicates that

☐   there will be an intersection with US Route 22 ahead

☐   the following exit is 22 miles away

☐   Exit 22 is just ahead

☐   Mileage 22 is up ahead

Question 114 - Road Signs

What does this sign mean?

- ☐ A winding road lies ahead
- ☐ A narrow bridge awaits you ahead
- ☐ There is a narrow road ahead
- ☐ There's a low clearance ahead

Question 115 - Road Signs

What does this sign mean?

- ☐ There will be two-way traffic ahead
- ☐ Lane crossing is permitted
- ☐ A one-way street awaits
- ☐ There will be an expressway or freeway ahead

Question 116 - Road Signs

This sign indicates that you are permitted to

☐   turn to the left

☐   make a right

☐   make a U-turn

☐   continue straight

Question 117 - Road Signs

What does this sign mean?

☐   You must proceed straight

☐   You must take a right

☐   You have the option of continuing straight or turning right

☐   You have the option of continuing straight or turning left

Question 118 - Road Signs

What exactly does this sign mean?

☐ You're headed in the wrong direction

☐ The road ahead has been closed

☐ A deserted road awaits you ahead

☐ You are not permitted to enter

Question 119 - Road Signs

What exactly does this sign mean?

☐ The lane is only for right turns

☐ The lane is shared by both directions of travel for left turns

☐ The lane is for high-speed vehicles only

☐ The lane is designated for specific purposes or vehicles

Question 120 - Road Signs

What exactly does this road sign mean?

☐ Continue straight

☐ It denotes the direction

☐ There is a rest area to the right

☐ Prepare to halt

Question 121 - Road Signs

What exactly does this sign mean?

☐ There is a traffic merging area ahead, please come to a complete stop before merging

☐ U-turns are permitted here, please drive slowly

☐ Proceed with caution as there is a one-way road ahead

☐ There will be a roundabout ahead, so be prepared to yield to traffic

Question 122 - Road Signs

What exactly does this sign mean?

○   At an intersection ahead, there is a traffic signal

○   A railroad crossing has a stop sign ahead

○   A stop sign at an intersection is ahead

○   None of the preceding

Question 123 - Road Signs

What exactly does this sign mean?

○   Beyond this sign, farm equipment is not permitted

○   A slick road awaits. use special tires

○   Farm machinery could be on the road

○   Vehicles must slow down as they approach a country road

Question 124 - Road Signs

What does this sign mean?

☐   Right-hand curve

☐   Turn sharply to the right

☐   There is no right turn

☐   Right-hand traffic merges

Question 125 - Road Signs

This posted sign can be found at

☐   intersections

☐   residential zones

☐   exit ramps from freeways

☐   crossings at schools

Question 126 - Road Signs

You have arrived at an intersection with this sign. When are you going to be able to turn right here?

☐   When no other vehicles are on the way

☐   Never

☐   When you see a green light or a green arrow

☐   When you come to a complete stop, yield to pedestrians and other vehicles

Question 127 - Road Signs

What does this sign mean?

☐   You're getting close to exit 444

☐   You're 444 miles from the state line and the end of the road

☐   You've arrived at Route 444

☐   It denotes none of the preceding

Question 128 - Road Signs

What does this signal indicate?

☐   You've arrived at an abandoned railroad track.

☐   You've arrived at a railroad crossing.

☐   There is a railroad track parallel to the road ahead.

☐   You've arrived at a train station.

Question 129 - Road Signs

This object is used as

☐   a reflector for the night

☐   a radar gun used by a cop

☐   a sign indicating an interstate route

☐   a traffic signal

Question 130 - Road Signs

The broken white lines on the road indicate that

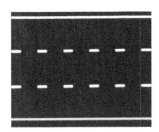

☐   there is no passing

☐   traffic flows in the opposite direction

☐   passing is permissible if done safely

☐   bicyclists and motorcyclists use the left lane

Question 131 - Road Signs

This symbol is used for

☐   indicating the path to a hospital

☐   displaying alternate routes in the event of road closures or construction

☐   displaying the designated routes

☐   displaying tourist routes

Question 132 - Road Signs

Which of the following pavement markings separates two lanes of traffic traveling in the same direction?

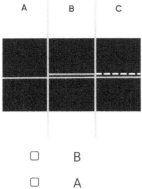

- ☐ B
- ☐ A
- ☐ C
- ☐ None of the preceding

Question 133 - Road Signs

What does this stop sign mean?

- ☐ Do not take a left or a straight path
- ☐ Continue straight
- ☐ Merge to the left
- ☐ Turn left or continue straight

Question 134 - Road Signs

This symbol indicates

☐ the road ahead is permanently closed.

☐ only people with disabilities are permitted to park.

☐ parking is not permitted.

☐ U-turns are not permitted.

Question 135 - Road Signs

What exactly does this sign mean?

☐ You need to change lanes

☐ You must proceed straight

☐ You must halt

☐ You must take a left

What exactly do these yellow pavement markings indicate?

☐   This is a three-way intersection

☐   Right turns are permitted for vehicles traveling in either direction

☐   Left turns are permitted for vehicles traveling in either direction

☐   It's a one-way street

Question 137 - Road Signs

This symbol is

☐   a stop symbol

☐   a yield symbol

☐   a sign that says 'Do Not Enter'

☐   a sign indicating a work zone

Question 138 - Road Signs

What exactly does this sign mean?

○ This lane allows you to turn left

○ From this lane, you must make a U-turn

○ You must proceed straight and detour at the intersection

○ You have the option of making a U-turn from this lane

Question 139 - Road Signs

What exactly does this sign mean?

○ There will be a traffic merge ahead, stop and then proceed

○ Except for buses, right lane exits

○ The road bends ahead, slow down to a safe speed

○ A narrow bridge lies ahead, proceed with caution

Question 140 - Road Signs

When is it legal to drive in a lane with this sign?

- ☐ If you need to get somewhere quickly
- ☐ Only if you have at least one passenger
- ☐ Only if you have at least two passengers
- ☐ If you are in charge of a truck

Question 141 - Road Signs

This road sign indicates

- ☐ there is a traffic light ahead
- ☐ there is a stop sign ahead
- ☐ there is a roundabout ahead
- ☐ there is a yield sign ahead

Question 142 - Road Signs

This regulatory symbol denotes

- ☐   a two-way street
- ☐   a right-turn lane with two lanes
- ☐   traffic merging in both directions
- ☐   a two-way left-turn lane

Question 143 - Road Signs

What exactly does this sign mean?

- ☐   There will be a work zone ahead of you
- ☐   There will be a hiccup in the road ahead
- ☐   There will be a low place in the road ahead
- ☐   There will be a detour ahead

Question 144 - Road Signs

This symbol indicates

☐   Vehicles must maintain a speed of at least 40 miles per hour

☐   Slow-moving vehicles are not permitted to exceed 40 mph

☐   Vehicles are not permitted to exceed the posted speed limit of 40 mph

☐   Vehicles must travel at a speed of fewer than 40 miles per hour

Question 145 - Road Signs

What do these two arrows represent?

☐   Start of a divided highway

☐   End of a divided highway

☐   Two-way traffic ahead

☐   Traffic to flow on both sides.

Question 146 - Road Signs

What exactly does this sign mean?

- ☐   There is a left turn ahead of you
- ☐   Turning left is not permitted
- ☐   A series of curves lie ahead
- ☐   A side road is entering from the right

Question 147 - Road Signs

What exactly does this sign mean?

- ☐   The speed limit posted for a sharp right turn
- ☐   The recommended minimum speed on a highway
- ☐   A safe speed indication for a right curve ahead.
- ☐   The speed limit posted for an S-shaped curve

Question 148 - Road Signs

The arrow on this sign indicates that

- ☐ drivers have the option of going in either direction
- ☐ all traffic must proceed only in the direction indicated by the arrow
- ☐ the lane ahead is designated for trucks turning right
- ☐ to make a right turn, all vehicles must come to a complete stop

Question 149 - Road Signs

If you see this sign and are traveling slower than the majority of traffic, you should

- ☐ accelerate your pace
- ☐ enter the left lane
- ☐ put yourself in the right lane
- ☐ take the next available exit

The availability of_____ is represented by this blue sign.

☐   food

☐   lodging

☐   gas station

☐   telephones

SITUATIONS AND SIGNS

Here you will find a collection of Signs and Situations that will help you sharpen your knowledge about intersections and shared lanes.

Total Questions: 50
Correct Answer to pass: 40

Question 1 - Signs and Situations

What exactly does this sign mean?

- ☐   A divided highway begins ahead of you

- ☐   There is a hazard ahead, proceed to the left or right

- ☐   At the next intersection, take a left or a right

- ☐   A Y-intersection is ahead

Question 2 - Signs and Situations

This symbol indicates

- ☐   there is a bridge ahead, the road width is 13 feet 6 inches

- ☐   parking area ahead, the road width is 13 feet 6 inches

- ☐   underpass ahead with a vertical clearance of 13 feet 6 inches

- ☐   there is a median ahead, the road width is 13 feet 6 inches

Question 3 - Signs and Situations

You've arrived at an intersection with a stop sign. Where must you draw the line?

☐ Before the crosswalk

☐ Before the stop line

☐ Before approaching the intersection

☐ Whichever of the aforementioned options you arrive at first

Question 4 - Signs and Situations

At around the same time, two cars arrive at an uncontrolled intersection (one without signs or signals). Which of the following statements is correct?

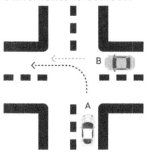

☐ Car A must yield to its right

☐ Due to Car A turning onto a new road, it has the right-of-way

☐ The drivers should decide who has the right of way

☐ Car B must yield to the right

Question 5 - Signs and Situations

Which of the following statements about headlights is NOT CORRECT?

☐ When using your windshield wipers continuously in bad weather, you must use your headlights

☐ From half an hour after sunset to half an hour before sunrise, you must use your headlights

☐ You may drive with your parking lights on to make your vehicle more visible

☐ When visibility is 500 feet or less, you must use your headlights

Question 6 - Signs and Situations

This road's center lane is separated from the other lanes by solid and broken yellow lines. This lane is intended for

☐ turning to the left

☐ parking

☐ passing

☐ emergency stops

Question 7 - Signs and Situations

What exactly does this sign mean?

- ☐ Slow down and proceed with caution because there is a school zone crossing ahead
- ☐ Prepare to stop at the crosswalk ahead
- ☐ Slow down and keep an eye out for pedestrians on the shared section of road ahead
- ☐ Slow down and keep an eye out for pedestrians as you approach a park or playground

Question 8 - Signs and Situations

You're following another car. What is the recommended minimum following distance behind the vehicle in front of you?

- ☐ 40 feet
- ☐ 2 seconds
- ☐ 4 seconds
- ☐ One car length, for every ten miles per hour of speed

Question 9 - Signs and Situations

A car has been parked in front of a fire hydrant. Is this legally allowed?

- ☐ No, you shouldn't park within 30 feet of a fire hydrant
- ☐ Yes, if it is moved within 10 minutes.
- ☐ Yes
- ☐ No, you are not permitted to park within 15 feet of a fire hydrant

Question 10 - Signs and Situations

This symbol indicates

- ☐ there is a double curve ahead
- ☐ there is a sharp right turn ahead
- ☐ there is a right-hand curve ahead
- ☐ a winding road lies ahead

Question 11 - Signs and Situations

What should you do if you see a steady yellow traffic light?

- ☐ Come to a halt, if it is safe to do so
- ☐ Proceed with caution because a hazard may be ahead
- ☐ Accelerate to clear the signal before it turns red
- ☐ Stop, yield to oncoming traffic and continue when it is safe to do so

Question 12 - Signs and Situations

You've arrived at a crossroads. You want to make a left and have a green light. Can you go ahead?

- ☐ Yes, because you will have the right-of-way
- ☐ Yes, but you must first yield to oncoming traffic and pedestrians
- ☐ No, you can only turn left when there is a green arrow
- ☐ Yes, but only if there is a sign indicating that a left turn is permitted

Question 13 - Signs and Situations

This driver is signaling with his hand. The driver plans to

- ○ accelerate
- ○ take a right.
- ○ take a left.
- ○ stop or slow down.

Question 14 - Signs and Situations

What does this sign mean?

- ○ Merging from the right
- ○ The conclusion of a divided highway
- ○ From the left, merge
- ○ Two-way street traffic

Question 15 - Signs and Situations

This driver is signaling with his hand. The driver plans to

- ☐ take a right
- ☐ take a left
- ☐ accelerate
- ☐ stop or slow down

Question 16 - Signs and Situations

What does this sign mean?

- ☐ There will be one-way traffic ahead
- ☐ The divided highway comes to an end ahead
- ☐ Traffic is congealing ahead
- ☐ A divided highway begins ahead of you

Question 17 - Signs and Situations

Which of the following railroad crossing statements is CORRECT?

☐ You must come to a complete stop at a flashing, red railroad signal until it is safe to proceed

☐ You may only drive through a rail cross gate if it is fully raised

☐ If you must stop at a railroad crossing, you must do so within 15-to-50 feet of the tracks

☐ All of the preceding statements are correct

Question 18 - Signs and Situations

When changing lanes, which of the following actions is optional?

☐ Examining your mirrors

☐ Signaling

☐ Checking behind your back

☐ None of the preceding

Question 19 - Signs and Situations

At about the same time, two cars arrive at a four-way stop. Which car should be the first to leave?

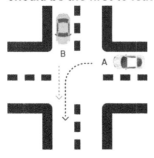

☐ Car B, as Car B is to the right of Car A

☐ Car A, because it is on the opposite side of the road from Car B

☐ As decided by the drivers

☐ Car A should go first, because it is turning onto a new road

Question 20 - Signs and Situations

On an open road, you notice a school bus stopped ahead, its red lights flashing and its stop arm extended. So, what should you do now?

☐ No matter which way you're going, come to a complete stop

☐ If you are traveling in the same direction as the school bus, you must come to a complete stop

☐ Reduce your speed to 10 mph and proceed with caution

☐ Stop, give way to pedestrians and then proceed cautiously

Question 21 - Signs and Situations

You're about to reach an intersection where you want to turn left. There are no other vehicles visible. Is it still necessary to signal?

☐ Yes, even if only briefly, you must use your turn signals

☐ Yes, you must turn on your turn signals at least 100 feet before making a turn

☐ No, turn signals are only required when other vehicles are present

☐ No, turn signals are not required

Question 22 - Signs and Situations

On a red light, you're about to make a right turn. A pedestrian begins to cross the road into which you intend to enter. So, what should you do now?

☐ Pass the pedestrian, merge into the far lane

☐ Alert the pedestrian to your presence, sound your horn

☐ Increase your speed to pass the pedestrian

☐ Allow the pedestrian to cross

Question 23 - Signs and Situations

You're in the right lane of a four-lane highway with a posted speed limit of 50 miles per hour. A police car with its lights flashing comes to a stop ahead of you. So, what should you do now?

☐ Proceed with extreme caution

☐ Reduce your speed to 35 mph or less and if possible, move into a non-adjacent lane

☐ If possible, move into a non-adjacent lane, otherwise, slow down to 35 mph or less

☐ Reduce your speed to 25 mph and proceed with caution

Question 24 - Signs and Situations

What does this sign mean?

☐ Vehicles in the left lane must make a left turn, while vehicles in the right lane must make a right turn

☐ Vehicles in the left lane must turn left, while those in the right lane must continue straight

☐ Vehicles in the left lane must merge left, while those in the right lane must merge right

☐ Vehicles in the left lane must turn left, while vehicles in the right lane may either continue straight or turn right

Question 25 - Signs and Situations

At about the same time, two cars arrive at an intersection. Which of the following statements is the most accurate?

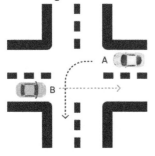

☐   Car A must yield because it is making a left turn

☐   Car B is required to yield to turning vehicles

☐   Due to Car A turning, it must yield

☐   The drivers must decide which of them will go first

Question 26 - Signs and Situations

Three cars arrive at an intersection just as some pedestrian crosses one of the roads. Who has the right of way in this situation?

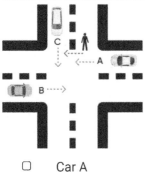

☐   Car A

☐   Car B

☐   Car C

☐   Pedestrian

Question 27 - Signs and Situations

You come to an intersection and see this sign. So, what should you do now?

☐ Stop completely, give way to pedestrians and traffic ahead and then proceed

☐ Maintain your speed because all traffic in front of you must yield to you

☐ Slow down and prepare to yield to oncoming traffic, but you will not be required to stop

☐ Slow down and prepare to yield to oncoming pedestrians and traffic

Question 28 - Signs and Situations

Which vehicles are hidden in the truck's blind spots (also known as 'No-Zones')?

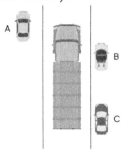

☐ Vehicle A

☐ Vehicle C

☐ Vehicles A and B

☐ Vehicle B

Question 29 - Signs and Situations

Two cars arrived at an intersection around the same time. Which of the following statements is correct?

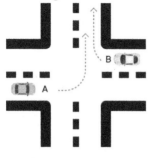

☐   Car A must yield because it is making a left turn.

☐   The first car has the right-of-way, the second car must then yield

☐   The other driver must be waved through by one of the drivers

☐   Due to Car B turning right, it must yield

Question 30 - Signs and Situations

A car is parked 15 feet from a railroad. Is this car parked legally?

☐   No, you are not permitted to park within 100 feet of a railroad crossing

☐   Yes, as long as you stay behind the stop line, you can park near a railroad crossing

☐   No, you are not permitted to park within 50 feet of a railroad crossing

☐   Yes, as long as you're not on the tracks, you can park near a railroad crossing

Question 31 - Signs and Situations

Which of the following statements about hydroplaning is correct?

☐ A gust of wind can cause a hydroplaning car to spin out of control

☐ At speeds as low as 35 mph, your tires can begin to hydroplane

☐ If your vehicle begins to hydroplane, you should slow down

☐ All of the preceding statements are correct

Question 32 - Signs and Situations

This driver is signaling with his hand. The driver intends to

☐ turn right

☐ stop or slow down

☐ accelerate

☐ take a left

Which of the following statements regarding railroad crossings is correct?

☐   A gate can be driven through before it is fully raised

☐   If you must stop, make sure you are at least 15 feet away from the tracks

☐   You can cross the tracks as soon as the train has passed if there is no fence

☐   All of the preceding statements are correct

What exactly does this sign mean?

☐   The top speed is 50 miles per hour

☐   The minimum speed limit is 50 miles per hour

☐   At night, the speed limit is 50 mph

☐   The recommended speed limit is 50 miles per hour

Question 35 - Signs and Situations

What exactly does this sign mean?

- ☐ A two-way, left-turn lane begins ahead of you
- ☐ The divided highway comes to an end ahead
- ☐ A divided highway begins ahead of you
- ☐ Ahead, left turns are not permitted

Question 36 - Signs and Situations

When is it legal to turn left at a red light?

- ☐ Never
- ☐ Only when turning from a one-way street onto another one-way street
- ☐ Only when turning from a one-way street onto a different street
- ☐ Unless otherwise stated, at any time

Question 37 - Signs and Situations

Is it legal to turn right at a red light?

- ☐ Yes, but only after coming to a complete stop and yielding to pedestrians and traffic
- ☐ Yes, because this is a 'protected' turn, you will have the right-of-way
- ☐ No, you cannot turn right at a red light
- ☐ Yes, but only if a sign permits you to

Question 38 - Signs and Situations

You parked on a steep incline with no curb. Which way should your front wheels be pointed?

☐   Towards the road's edge

☐   Straight

☐   Away from the road's edge

☐   Any direction is possible

Question 39 - Signs and Situations

Two vehicles are making a left turn onto a divided highway. Which vehicles are turning properly?

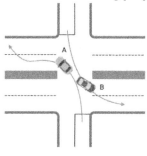

☐   Vehicle B

☐   Both automobiles

☐   Vehicle A

☐   Neither vehicle

Question 40 - Signs and Situations

What should you do if you see a flashing red light?

☐   Yield in the same way that you would at a yield sign

☐   Stop and yield as if at a stop sign

☐   Proceed with caution. this signal has been deactivated

☐   Stop and hold your breath until the red light stops flashing

Question 41 - Signs and Situations

You come to a stop at a crossroads with a green traffic signal. You want to drive straight through the intersection. Which of the following statements is correct?

☐ You are unable to proceed

☐ You may proceed after yielding to any traffic already in the intersection

☐ You are free to continue

☐ You must first come to a complete stop and yield before proceeding

Question 42 - Signs and Situations

What exactly does this sign mean?

☐ Trucks transporting dangerous materials may enter the road

☐ Heavy vehicles may enter the road

☐ Fire trucks may have to enter the road

☐ Farm vehicles might enter the roadway

Question 43 - Signs and Situations

Car B has entered an intersection to make a right turn on a red light. Car A has a green light and wishes to proceed through the intersection. Which of the following statements is correct?

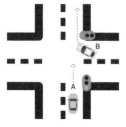

☐   Car A should accelerate to pass Car B

☐   Car A must give way to Car B

☐   Car B must come to a halt and allow Car A to pass

☐   None of the preceding statements is correct.

Question 44 - Signs and Situations

You notice an emergency vehicle approaching with flashing lights. So, what should you do now?

☐   Take it easy

☐   Accelerate and look for a safe place to turn off

☐   Pull over to the side of the road and come to a complete stop

☐   Keep your speed and direction constant

Question 45 - Signs and Situations

What exactly does this sign mean?

- ☐ At night, the speed limit is 35 mph

- ☐ During the day, the speed limit is 35 mph

- ☐ The top speed is 35 miles per hour

- ☐ The recommended speed limit is 35 miles per hour

Question 46 - Signs and Situations

Whom should you yield before turning left into a driveway?

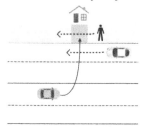

- ☐ Pedestrians and oncoming traffic

- ☐ Oncoming traffic, but not pedestrians

- ☐ Oncoming vehicles, but not pedestrians

- ☐ Neither pedestrians nor oncoming vehicles.

Question 47 - Signs and Situations

You've parked next to a curb and are facing uphill. Which way should your front wheels be pointed?

☐ Any possible direction

☐ Away from the curb

☐ Towards the curb

☐ Straight

Question 48 - Signs and Situations

When must you dim your high-beam headlights?

☐ When you're within 1,000 feet of another vehicle

☐ Whenever you are within 500 feet of an oncoming vehicle or within 200 feet of another vehicle which you are following

☐ Whenever you are within 200 feet of an oncoming vehicle or within 500 feet of another vehicle which you are following

☐ When you're within 500 feet of another vehicle

Question 49 - Signs and Situations

You come to an intersection and see this sign. So, what should you do now?

☐ Before proceeding, come to a complete stop and yield to traffic

☐ Come to a complete stop before proceeding

☐ You can't go through here, find another way

☐ Reduce your speed and proceed only if the intersection is clear

Which of the following commands has precedence (i.e., should be followed above all others)?

☐ A cautionary sign

☐ A STOP indication

☐ A traffic light

☐ A police officer

FINES & LIMITS

This section is specific to your State and you will find 10 questions on Fines and Limits here. It is one of the most difficult sections and the one that most people fail.

Total Questions: 10
Correct Answer to pass: 8

Question 1 - Fines & Limits

The person who is most typically killed in an alcohol-related crash is

- ☐   a passenger in the backseat
- ☐   a young passenger
- ☐   the impaired driver
- ☐   the other vehicle's driver

Question 2 - Fines & Limits

If a Minnesota driver under the age of 21 is convicted of DWI, his or her license will be suspended for _____ days.

- ☐   60
- ☐   180
- ☐   30
- ☐   90

Question 3 - Fines & Limits

If you are convicted of driving an uninsured vehicle, you might spend up to _____ days in jail.

- ☐ 180
- ☐ 30
- ☐ 90
- ☐ 60

Question 4 - Fines & Limits

A first offense of DWI can result in _____ days in jail and/or a _____ fine.

- ☐ 30; $100
- ☐ 90; $1,000
- ☐ 60; $250
- ☐ 90; $500

Question 5 - Fines & Limits

You will be eligible for a work permit _____, after your first DWI conviction.

- ☐ after a 15-day revocation period has passed
- ☐ if your blood alcohol concentration (BAC) was below 0.16%
- ☐ after you meet all reinstatement requirements
- ☐ If all of the preceding statements are correct

Question 6 - Fines & Limits

A fourth DWI conviction within ten years may result in the loss of driving privileges for up to _____ years.

- ☐ 2
- ☐ 4
- ☐ 3
- ☐ 5

Question 7 - Fines & Limits

If you are convicted of an offense in another state that would have resulted in the revocation of your Minnesota driver's license,

- ☐ you'll need to take a driver's education course
- ☐ your driver's license will be revoked
- ☐ you'll have to pay a large fine
- ☐ your driver's license will be unaffected

Question 8 - Fines & Limits

Which of the following may result in the suspension of your license?

- ☐ Repeatedly breaking traffic laws
- ☐ Having a fake driver's license
- ☐ Failure to pay a traffic fine when necessary
- ☐ Everything mentioned above

Question 9 - Fines & Limits

If you are convicted of exceeding 100 mph while driving, your driver's license will be revoked for

☐ thirty days

☐ two years

☐ six months

☐ one year

Question 10 - Fines & Limits

Minnesota law forbids driving while impaired by

☐ prescription drugs

☐ household products used as inhalants

☐ illegal drugs

☐ all of the aforementioned

DISTRACTED DRIVING TEST

This is one of the most crucial sections. You'll be asked about modern driving distractions, as well as, driving while under the influence of drugs and pharmaceuticals.

Total Questions: 25
Correct Answer to pass: 20

Question 1 - Distracted Driving

You should be cautious of the various distractions and limitations listed below -

- ☐ Listening to extremely loud music or using technologies like cell phones, GPS and intercoms
- ☐ Changing your vehicle's electronic controls
- ☐ Alcohol, drugs and some medications
- ☐ Everything mentioned above

Question 2 - Distracted Driving

What other medications, besides alcohol, can impair a person's ability to drive safely?

- ☐ Medications available over-the-counter
- ☐ Prescribed medication
- ☐ Medications used to treat headaches, colds, hay fever or other allergies, as well as, those used to relax the nerves
- ☐ Everything mentioned above

Question 3 - Distracted Driving

You're behind the wheel and a problem in the rear seat requires your attention. You must:

☐ Turn around and cope with the situation, occasionally looking ahead

☐ Before dealing with the matter, pull over to the side of the road and park your vehicle

☐ Adjust the rearview mirror to see what's in the back seat

☐ Slow down and deal with the matter while you're driving

Question 4 - Distracted Driving

Which of the following will NOT keep you from being distracted while driving?

☐ You could save your favorite radio stations by pre-programming them

☐ Pre-loosening the lid of your coffee cup

☐ Pre-planning your trip

☐ Before you begin, make sure that all of your mirrors are adjusted

Question 5 - Distracted Driving

What should you do if you feel drowsy before driving?

☐ Listen to music

☐ Coffee Drinking

☐ Exercise

☐ Sleeping

Question 6 - Distracted Driving

Drivers must _____ to keep awake when driving to overcome highway hypnosis, drowsiness and tiredness.

- ☐ Take stimulants
- ☐ Use the cell phone
- ☐ Message someone
- ☐ Exercise the eyes

Question 7 - Distracted Driving

Which of the following is NOT an adequate way to drive?

- ☐ Using visual, display gadgets and texting while driving
- ☐ When driving, use side mirrors
- ☐ Listening to music while driving
- ☐ While parking, look both front and sideways

Question 8 - Distracted Driving

Is it legal for teenage drivers to talk on their cell phones while driving?

- ☐ Only when traveling at less than 25 mph
- ☐ Yes, as long as you're cautious
- ☐ It is illegal to talk on a cell phone while driving
- ☐ Only if you're on a country road

Question 9 - Distracted Driving

You don't want to be a distracted driver, therefore

☐ when there are no other vehicles around you, browse maps or use your phone

☐ turn off your phone till you get to your location

☐ have all of your highly emotional conversations during the first hour of driving

☐ smoke, eat and drink, on straight sections of the road

Question 10 - Distracted Driving

Which of the statements below is correct?

☐ It is safe and time-saving to have lunch while driving

☐ While driving, you can send and read brief texts

☐ If you get lost while driving, you can rapidly write navigation instructions

☐ Using audio navigation while driving is legal

Question 11 - Distracted Driving

Can you take drugs before getting behind the wheel?

☐ Only with a prescription

☐ No

☐ Only over-the-counter medications

☐ Only if the doctor believes it won't impair your ability to drive safely

Question 12 - Distracted Driving

Talking on a cell phone while driving increases your chances of getting involved in a crash by:

- ☐ Up to twice as much
- ☐ An additional sum
- ☐ Up to three times as much
- ☐ As much as four times

Question 13 - Distracted Driving

Is it safe to drive while holding something in your lap?

- ☐ Never, ever
- ☐ Yes, as long as it's not a human or a pet
- ☐ Yes, if it's a small animal
- ☐ Yes, as long as you don't get distracted

Question 14 - Distracted Driving

Things that can keep you from paying attention to the road include:

- ☐ Texting and talking on the phone
- ☐ Checking blind spots
- ☐ Checking the traffic behind you regularly
- ☐ Always looking in the mirror

Question 15 - Distracted Driving

Is it illegal to text while driving?

    ☐   Yes, it is illegal

    ☐   It's legal as long as you don't go faster than 15 mph

    ☐   No, it is legal

    ☐   Only when you come to a complete stop at a stop sign, is it legal

Question 16 - Distracted Driving

Which medicines can impair your ability to drive safely?

    ☐   Medications available over-the-counter

    ☐   Illegal drugs

    ☐   Prescription medications

    ☐   Everything mentioned above

Question 17 - Distracted Driving

Which of the following statements about cell phones is correct?

    ☐   If you get a call while driving, slow down and take the call

    ☐   Adult drivers are permitted to use a hands-free cell phone while driving

    ☐   Adult drivers are permitted to use a hand-held cell phone while driving

    ☐   Calling while driving saves time

Question 18 - Distracted Driving

A juvenile driver receives a phone call on his or her cell phone. He or she must:

☐ Not carry a cell phone when driving.

☐ Answer the phone in an emergency

☐ Not pick up the phone

☐ Answer the phone, utilizing a hands-free cell phone.

Question 19 – Distracted Driving

How can sleep deprivation affect your driving?

☐ Impaired decision-making

☐ Slower response times

☐ Reduced awareness

☐ Everything mentioned above

Question 20 - Distracted Driving

Which of these will not negatively impact your driving while you're on the road?

☐ Listening to the radio

☐ Drinking coffee

☐ Smoking

☐ Eating a sandwich

DRINKING AND DRIVING TEST

This section discusses the consequences of drinking and driving. Be sure to understand the limitations and the effects of alcohol on your body.

Total Questions: 25
Correct Answer to pass: 20

Question 1 - Drinking and Driving

Which of the following is prohibited for minors?

☐ Having a blood alcohol concentration (BAC) of 0.02 percent or higher

☐ Attempting to buy alcohol

☐ Drinking alcohol

☐ Everything mentioned above

Question 2 - Drinking and Driving

Which of the following has the most alcohol?

☐ A 5-oz glass of 12% wine

☐ A 1.5-oz shot of 80 proof liquor

☐ A 12-oz glass of 5% beer

☐ They're all the same

Question 3 - Drinking and Driving

Which of the following areas does not allow open containers of alcohol?

☐ Passenger areas of standard passenger cars

☐ Passenger areas of limousines

☐ In the trunk of a passenger car

☐ Residential areas of motorhomes

Question 4 - Drinking and Driving

Alcohol might have an impact on your

☐ concentration

☐ reaction time

☐ decision-making process

☐ all of the answers above are correct

Question 5 - Drinking and Driving

_____ is the biggest cause of death among Americans aged 16 to 24.

☐ Driving while under the influence of alcohol

☐ Cancer

☐ Obesity

☐ Overdose from drugs

Question 6 - Drinking and Driving

_____ impacts your blood alcohol concentration (BAC)?

- ☐ The number of alcoholic beverages you've consumed
- ☐ How quickly you drink
- ☐ How much you weigh
- ☐ Everything mentioned above

Question 7 - Drinking and Driving

Which of the following beverages has a 1.5-ounce amount of alcohol?

- ☐ 1 liter of beer
- ☐ One shot of 80 proof liquor
- ☐ A 5-oz. glass of wine
- ☐ Each of the above

Question 8 - Drinking and Driving

It is especially risky to drink alcohol and drive at night because:

- ☐ At night, the roadways are crowded
- ☐ Your field of vision is already limited
- ☐ At night, drinking has a greater impact on your judgment
- ☐ You are more likely to encounter drunk drivers

Question 9 - Drinking and Driving

A drunk motorist is more likely to:

- ☐ Drive too quickly or too slowly
- ☐ Frequently change lanes
- ☐ Fail to dim high lights for oncoming traffic
- ☐ Do all of the above.

Question 10 - Drinking and Driving

Which of the following occurs when a driver's blood alcohol concentration (BAC) rises?

☐ Alcohol impairs coordination and muscle control

☐ The first processes to be impacted are self-control and judgment

☐ Alcohol has a growing impact on the brain of the drinker

☐ All of the aforementioned

Question 11 - Drinking and Driving

Which of the following will assist a person under the influence of alcohol in recovering from the effects?

☐ Time

☐ Cold, fresh air

☐ A mug of coffee

☐ Everything mentioned above

Question 12 - Drinking and Driving

The concept of implied consent states that by operating a motor vehicle, you have accepted that

☐ if a police officer requests it, you will submit to a chemical test

☐ you will never drink alcohol or have an open bottle or other container containing alcohol while driving

☐ you will always follow the fundamental rules

☐ none of the above applies to you

Question 13 - Drinking and Driving

It is unlawful to have open containers of alcohol in a car in which of the following places?

☐ Beneath the seat

☐ The first-row seating

☐ The console

☐ All of the preceding

Question 14 - Drinking and Driving

Which of the following is NOT an alcohol effect?

☐ Erroneous judgment

☐ Vision impairment

☐ Slower reaction times

☐ Increased vigilance

Question 15 - Drinking and Driving

Driving and drinking

☐ diminishes your reflexes

☐ reduces a driver's awareness of potential hazards on the road

☐ reduces physical control of a vehicle

☐ does everything mentioned above

Question 16 - Drinking and Driving

Which of the following is an acceptable substitute for drinking and driving?

- ☐ Public transports
- ☐ A designated driver
- ☐ A taxicab
- ☐ Any of the preceding

Question 17 - Drinking and Driving

If you are convicted of driving under the influence of alcohol or drugs, you may face the penalties listed below.

- ☐ Community service
- ☐ Suspension of your driver's license
- ☐ Severe fines and increased insurance rates
- ☐ Any or all of the preceding

Question 18 - Drinking and Driving

Which of the following statements about drivers under the age of twenty-one is correct?

- ☐ They are permitted to consume small amounts of alcohol, but not while driving
- ☐ They can purchase alcohol but are not permitted to consume it
- ☐ They are permitted to have trace levels of alcohol in their blood while driving
- ☐ They are not permitted to purchase, consume or be in possession of alcohol

Question 19 - Drinking and Driving

How many standard servings of alcohol can an adult safely drink before driving?

☐   2

☐   It depends on the person

☐   1

☐   3

Question 20 - Drinking and Driving

Which of the following is an effect of drinking on your ability to drive?

☐   Reduces driving ability

☐   It slows reflexes

☐   It negatively impacts one's depth perception

☐   Everything mentioned above

Question 21 - Drinking and Driving

Which of the following has no effect on blood alcohol content?

☐   Body mass index

☐   The type of alcohol

☐   Timespan during which alcohol was consumed

☐   Length of time since the last drink

Question 22 - Drinking and Driving

Which of the below will result in a required suspension of a minor's license?

- ☐ Transporting an open beer container
- ☐ Driving while under the influence of drugs
- ☐ Transporting an open container of alcohol
- ☐ Any or all of the preceding

Question 23 - Drinking and Driving

After drinking a significant amount of alcohol, you can ensure that you will not be driving under the influence if you

- ☐ drank beer or wine but no strong liquor
- ☐ wait at least an hour
- ☐ wait a day or two
- ☐ wait at least 30 minutes

Question 24 - Drinking and Driving

If you are unable to drive your vehicle because of excessive alcohol consumption, you must

- ☐ allow a designated driver to operate your vehicle
- ☐ keep yourself awake when driving by drinking coffee
- ☐ call 911 for assistance with driving
- ☐ before driving, utilize medications to counteract the effects of alcohol

Question 25 - Drinking and Driving

Your driving privileges may be suspended

    ☐   if you refuse to take a blood or urine test

    ☐   if you transport alcoholic beverages in closed containers while working for someone, who has an off-site liquor sales license

    ☐   if you have a full, sealed, unopened container of liquor, beer or wine in your vehicle

    ☐   if you do not appoint a sober driver

EXAM TEST PRACTICE

Welcome to the final part of this book, sit down, relax and get focused. This practice test contains the same number of questions you will find in your official DMV exam.

Total Questions: 40
Correct Answer to pass: 32

Question 1 - Mock Exam

You should signal for at least _____ feet before turning left.

☐   200

☐   100

☐   50

☐   25

Question 2 - Mock Exam

What should you do if the fog becomes so dense that you can't see?

☐   To avoid glare, use fog lights

☐   Extend your following distance

☐   Drive at a speed of no more than 10 mph and switch on your hazard lights

☐   Pull over on the side of the road and wait for visibility to improve

Question 3 - Mock Exam

Is it permissible to turn right on a red arrow pointing right?

☐ Yes, but only after you've given way to pedestrians and other traffic

☐ No

☐ Yes, but only if no other vehicles are approaching

☐ Yes, but only after you've come to a complete stop

Question 4 - Mock Exam

What exactly is a "no zone"?

☐ A parking zone where you are not permitted to park

☐ One of the blind spots of your vehicle

☐ A school district

☐ A commercial vehicle's blind spot

Question 5 - Mock Exam

When parallel parking close to a curb, your vehicle must be parked no further than _____ from the curb.

☐ 2 feet

☐ 20 inches

☐ 12 inches

☐ 3 feet

When a school bus comes to a complete stop with its red lights flashing and its stop arm extended, what should you do?

☐ No matter which way you're going, come to a complete stop

☐ If you are traveling in the same direction as the bus, you must come to a complete stop

☐ If you spot schoolchildren, slow down and prepare to stop

☐ Only stop if the bus stopped is in a school zone

What is the best strategy to avoid colliding with another vehicle if it suddenly cuts in front of you?

☐ Sound your horn

☐ Swerve into the next lane

☐ Firmly apply the brakes

☐ Take your foot off the gas pedal

What does a double solid yellow line denote?

☐ It is permissible to pass

☐ There are two lanes of traffic traveling in the same direction

☐ A road barrier

☐ A no-passage zone

Question 9 - Mock Exam

Parking is prohibited within _____ feet of a fire hydrant in Minnesota.

- ☐ 20
- ☐ 15
- ☐ 10
- ☐ 25

Question 10 - Mock Exam

When is it permissible to send text messages on a hand-held cell phone while driving, according to the Minnesota Driver's Manual?

- ☐ If you are at least 21 years old
- ☐ If you are unable to make a voice call
- ☐ If you're not in a residential area
- ☐ Never

Question 11 - Mock Exam

A center turn lane could be deployed for

- ☐ left turns only
- ☐ left turns and backing up
- ☐ U-turns, left turns, and passing
- ☐ passing

Question 12 - Mock Exam

You should _____ before changing lanes.

☐   look over your shoulder

☐   examine your blind spots

☐   examine your mirrors

☐   complete all of the preceding tasks

Question 13 - Mock Exam

When passing a bicycle heading in your direction in Minnesota, you must allow at least _____ of space between the side of your vehicle and the bicycle.

☐   6 feet

☐   5 feet

☐   3 feet

☐   10 feet

Question 14 - Mock Exam

When you're going to turn left at a green signal, you notice a pedestrian in the crosswalk. Who has the right-of-way here?

☐   Your vehicle, because vehicles have the right-of-way at all times

☐   Your vehicle, because the light is green

☐   The pedestrian, because the light is green

☐   The pedestrian, because pedestrians have the right-of-way at all times

Question 15 - Mock Exam

When should you give a signal before passing the vehicle in front of you?

☐ Always

☐ Only when there are vehicles in front of you.

☐ If you are unsure whether the driver of the vehicle is aware that you want to pass

☐ On multi-lane highways with more than two lanes

Question 16 - Mock Exam

A diamond-symbolized lane may be

☐ a lane for turning

☐ a passing lane

☐ a high-occupancy vehicle (HOV) lane

☐ an exit ramp

Question 17 - Mock Exam

How many lanes should you switch at once?

☐ Two

☐ One

☐ More than three

☐ Three

Question 18 - Mock Exam

Wet roads are dangerous because

☐   it is possible that your tires will lose touch with the road

☐   traffic lights may fail

☐   your engine may become overly moist

☐   your view may be obstructed by the windshield wipers

Question 19 - Mock Exam

When is it permissible to pass through lowered railroad crossing gates?

☐   When you notice that the train has gone

☐   Never

☐   At light rail crossings

☐   If you are certain that no trains are approaching

Question 20 - Mock Exam

When you are within _____ feet of an oncoming vehicle, you must dim your headlights to low beam.

☐   200

☐   500

☐   300

☐   1000

Question 21 - Mock Exam

When waiting at an intersection to make a left turn, _____.

☐   continue to turn your wheels to the left

☐   change gears

☐   keep your wheels straight

☐   continue to turn your wheels to the right

Question 22 - Mock Exam

The sole remedy for carbon monoxide poisoning is

☐   application of ice

☐   a couple of glasses of water

☐   application of heat

☐   a sufficient amount of fresh air

Question 23 - Mock Exam

You see a bicycle on your left has arrived ahead of you as you approach an uncontrolled intersection (one without signs or signals). Who has the right-of-way here?

☐   You, because you're on the right side of the bicycle

☐   Because it's to your left, it's the bicycle

☐   You, because bicycles must defer to automobiles

☐   The bicycle, because it was the first to come

Question 24 - Mock Exam

When turning left from a one-way street onto a two-way street, begin your turn in

☐ the right lane

☐ the left lane

☐ the middle lane

☐ any lane

Question 25 - Mock Exam

When you can't see well for at least _____ feet ahead, turn on your headlights.

☐ 100

☐ 500

☐ 1000

☐ 250

Question 26 - Mock Exam

Work zones often have

☐ increased speed limits

☐ a normal speed restriction of 10 miles per hour

☐ lowered speed limits

☐ no speed limits

Question 27 - Mock Exam

When parking your vehicle facing downhill, point the front wheels toward the curb. What else can you do?

- ☐ Activate the hazard lights
- ☐ Check your mirrors
- ☐ Apply the parking brake
- ☐ Complete all the preceding tasks

Question 28 - Mock Exam

Traffic lanes heading in the same direction are divided by

- ☐ solid or dashed (broken) white lines
- ☐ dashed (broken) yellow lines
- ☐ double yellow lines
- ☐ solid yellow lines

Question 29 - Mock Exam

You must make a right turn in

- ☐ the right lane
- ☐ the left lane
- ☐ whatever lane is most convenient for your travel plans
- ☐ whichever lane interferes with traffic the least

Question 30 - Mock Exam

You are at a stop sign, ready to turn right. A vehicle coming from the left has its turn signal activated. So, what should you do now?

☐   Turn ahead since the other vehicle is about to turn as well

☐   Turn on your headlights as soon as possible

☐   Wait until the other vehicle begins to turn before beginning your turn

☐   Immediately press the accelerator (gas pedal)

Question 31 - Mock Exam

Which of the following pavement markings assertions is baseless?

☐   To make a left turn into or out of an alley, you may cross a double solid yellow line

☐   Dashed (broken) yellow lines separate traffic lanes traveling in opposite directions

☐   On a roadway, it is legal to cross a double solid white line

☐   White lines that are dashed (broken) separate lanes of vehicles traveling in the same direction

Question 32 - Mock Exam

If you see a yield sign, it means you should slow down and prepare to _____ if a vehicle or pedestrian is approaching from the opposite direction.

☐   turn

☐   stop

☐   make a U-turn

☐   increase your speed

Question 33 - Mock Exam

If your parked car rolls away and collides with another unattended vehicle, you should

- ☐   remove your car and park at a more secure location

- ☐   inform the police about the incident

- ☐   repair the other vehicle

- ☐   remove your car and continue your journey

Question 34 - Mock Exam

If you see an old person crossing a street, you should

- ☐   increase your speed and cross the junction as soon as possible

- ☐   continue driving

- ☐   come to a complete stop and yield the right-of-way

- ☐   honk your horn

Question 35 - Mock Exam

You should _____ and keep an eye out for oncoming traffic before reaching the crest of a hill or entering a curve.

- ☐   slow down, move to the right side of the road

- ☐   slow down, move to the left side of the road

- ☐   speed up, turn on your headlights

- ☐   speed up, shift gears

Question 36 - Mock Exam

Which of the following headlight claims is incorrect?

☐ Low beams are used when traveling in cities and while stuck in traffic

☐ When there is no traffic in sight, high lights are employed in open country driving

☐ When going behind other vehicles, high lights are used

☐ When driving in fog, rain, or snow, low beams are used

Question 37 - Mock Exam

If you're traveling down a steep incline, you should

☐ take off your seat belt

☐ switch on your headlights

☐ firmly push the brake pedal

☐ change to a lower gear

Question 38 - Mock Exam

In order to avoid a head-on collision, If an oncoming vehicle is in your lane, you should

☐ maintain a straight grip on the steering wheel

☐ accelerate your pace

☐ take a left turn toward the median

☐ steer to the right, toward the shoulder, or the curb

Vehicles from either direction can make _____ from the center lane on a two-way roadway with a center lane.

- ☐ U-turns
- ☐ frequent stops
- ☐ left turns
- ☐ right turns

Question 40 - Mock Exam

You're driving through a roundabout. An emergency vehicle with a siren, an air horn, or a flashing red or blue light is approaching. So, what should you do now?

- ☐ Pull over to the right in the roundabout
- ☐ Pull over to the left in the roundabout
- ☐ Continue until you reach your exit, then turn right
- ☐ Stop in the middle of the roundabout

ANSWER SHEETS

DIAGNOSTIC TEST

Question 1 - Diagnostic Test

(D) The reinstatement fee is $30 if you lost your driver's license for a reason other than DWI or unlawful vehicular operation. [Reinstatement Fees, Minnesota Driver's Manual, Chapter 1 Your License to Drive]

Question 2 - Diagnostic Test

(B) This is an object marker sign, which is used to alert drivers about things in the road or extremely close to the road's edge. The stripes point down the road, toward the safe side. This sign advises that you should continue to the right in order to pass the object.

Question 3 - Diagnostic Test

(D) If you deny chemical testing for alcohol or drug use, your driver's license will be suspended for one to six years, depending on the number of past convictions. [Implied Consent Law, Chapter 8 of the Minnesota Driver's Manual, Driving Under the Influence of Alcohol or Drugs]

Question 4 - Diagnostic Test

(C) This sign warns that there will be a double curve ahead. The road ahead bends to the right, then to the left. (A winding road sign would be posted instead if there was a triple curve coming.) Slow down, stay to the right, and do not pass.

Question 5 - Diagnostic Test

(C) There are unique restrictions that must be followed when driving on painted curbs. In Minnesota, you are not permitted to park on a yellow-painted curb. You can, however, make a brief stop there to pick up or drop off products or passengers. It should be noted that there is no national standard for curb colors. Each state may have its own set of rules. Always verify the local traffic laws when going out of state.

Question 6 - Diagnostic Test

(C) Lane use control signals are special overhead signals that indicate which lanes of a roadway may be used in various directions at different times. A flashing yellow "X" indicates that this lane is solely for left turns. Use caution because oncoming vehicles turning left may also use this lane.

Question 7 - Diagnostic Test

(D) On four-lane divided highways, reduced conflict crossings are meant to lower the number of collisions. Drivers always make a right turn followed by a U-turn at a reduced conflict intersection. When approaching the split highway from a side street, motorists are not permitted to make left turns or cross traffic; instead, they must turn right onto the highway and then make a U-turn at a designated median opening.

Question 8 - Diagnostic Test

(D) When an emergency vehicle (ambulance, fire truck, police car, etc.) with flashing red lights and a siren or bell approaches you on a two-way road, you must draw to the right and come to a complete stop. If you are traveling on a one-way road, you must pull over to the nearest side and halt. However, even if an emergency vehicle is approaching, you must not block a junction. If you get to an intersection, go straight through it and then pull over. Continue to stand still until all emergency vehicles have passed.

Question 9 - Diagnostic Test

(B) A reflective triangular symbol on the rear of a vehicle marks it as a slow-moving vehicle, as defined by Minnesota as one that cannot exceed 30 mph. (These vehicles include horse-drawn carriages and various farm machinery.) Slow down or prepare to change lanes when you approach one of these vehicles.

Question 10 - Diagnostic Test

(A) When you use the lap and shoulder belts together, you have a better chance of surviving a car accident. Adjust the lap belt so that it fits tightly across your hip bones or upper thighs. It should never be placed over your abdomen or on the soft region of your stomach. The shoulder belt should be snugly worn over your chest and across the middle of your shoulder.

Question 11 - Diagnostic Test

(D) Using a motor vehicle to flee a police officer on official duty is a felony in Minnesota. The penalty is imprisonment for no more than three years and one day, a $5,000 fine, or both.

Question 12 - Diagnostic Test

(C) Towing a camper or trailer requires a following distance of at least 500 feet from other vehicles.

Question 13 - Diagnostic Test

(B) When passing another vehicle, you must return to the right side of the road before approaching an oncoming vehicle within 100 feet. (Even the legal minimum distance is a bit short.) If your vehicle and the approaching vehicle are both moving at 40 mph, the two vehicles will close a 100-foot gap in less than one second before colliding head-on.)

Question 14 - Diagnostic Test

(B) A steady yellow indication indicates that the signal is soon to turn red. If you are approaching an intersection, you must stop if it is safe to do so. If this is not the case, proceed with caution.

Question 15 - Diagnostic Test

(C) Most freeway entrance ramps have an acceleration lane that allows you to increase your speed to highway traffic speed before merging.

PRACTICE TEST 1

Question 1 - Practice Test 1
(C) Yellow lines are also utilized as left-edge lines on one-way streets.

Question 2 - Practice Test 1
(D) When you drive too fast on a wet road, you may experience hydroplaning. If your vehicle begins to hydroplane, do not apply the brakes. Braking too hard may cause your vehicle to slip out of control. Instead, remove your foot from the accelerator and allow your car to slow down until hydroplaning ceases.

Question 3 - Practice Test 1
(A) For entering freeways, entrance ramps are provided. Typically, the entrance ramp leads to an acceleration lane. Increase your speed as you approach and enter the acceleration lane to match the vehicles in the through lanes. Keep an eye out for an opening in freeway traffic, activate your turn signal and merge smoothly with the rest of the traffic. Unless absolutely necessary, do not stop or slow down in the acceleration lane.

Question 4 - Practice Test 1
(D) Vehicles approaching from a private road or driveway must come to a complete stop and yield to vehicles on public roads.

Question 5 - Practice Test 1
(C) When you wear a lap and shoulder belt together, your chances of getting seriously wounded in a crash are considerably reduced. The lap belt covers your lower body and prevents ejection from the car. Your head and chest are protected by the shoulder belt from colliding with the dashboard or windshield.

Question 6 - Practice Test 1
(A) Turn on your low-beam headlights to improve visibility in fog, rain or snow. High beams can produce glare by reflecting off precipitation.

Question 7 - Practice Test 1
(A) When (1) the vehicle is making or about to make a left turn, or (2) there are two or more lanes of traffic traveling in the same direction as you, you may pass on the right. (On a multilane highway or a one-way street, this could be the case.)

Question 8 - Practice Test 1
(D) According to statistics, 30 percent of traffic fatalities are caused by striking the steering assembly, while another 40 percent are caused by impacting the windshield, windshield frame or instrument panel. Wearing a lap/shoulder belt significantly minimizes your chances of being killed in a crash. The lap belt covers your lower body and prevents ejection. The shoulder belt prevents your head and chest from colliding with the steering column or windshield.

Question 9 - Practice Test 1
(D) Don't stop, back up or try to turn around if you miss your exit on a

freeway. This greatly increases the possibility of a collision. Instead, proceed to the next exit and find a way to return from there.

Question 10 - Practice Test 1
(A) The driver of the vehicle on the left must yield to the driver of the vehicle on the right, when two cars enter an uncontrolled intersection (one that is not regulated by signs or signals) from different highways, at roughly the same time.

Question 11 - Practice Test 1
(B) At intersections and crosswalks, you must yield the right-of-way to pedestrians.

Question 12 - Practice Test 1
(C) You must get clear of any intersection, pull over to the curb or side of the road and come to a complete stop if an emergency vehicle with flashing red or blue lights and a siren approaches from either direction.

Question 13 - Practice Test 1
(D) Bicycles must abide by the same traffic laws as other vehicles. When approaching an uncontrolled intersection (one without traffic signs or signals), yield to the vehicle or bicycle that arrives first. If other vehicles or bicycles arrive around the same time, you must yield to the one on your right.

Question 14 - Practice Test 1
(A) Do not spend time in a no-zone. No-Zones are wide regions around trucks, buses and other large vehicles where cars may disappear into blind spots or get too close to prevent the truck driver from properly stopping or maneuvering. To the front, back and sides of the vehicle, there are no-zones. It is impossible to totally avoid the no-zones created by a heavy truck. However, do not stay in a no-zone for any longer than is necessary to pass the vehicle safely and never tailgate a truck.

Question 15 - Practice Test 1
(B) When the road is wet, worn or bald tires, can increase stopping distance and make turning more difficult. Unbalanced tires or low tire pressures can result in faster tire wear and reduced fuel economy, as well as, making the vehicle more difficult to steer and stop.

Question 16 - Practice Test 1
(D) For entering freeways, entrance ramps are available. Typically, the entrance ramp leads to an acceleration lane. Increase your speed to match that of the vehicles in the through lanes as you approach and enter the acceleration lane. Keep an eye out for a gap in the motorway traffic, engage your turn signal and join gently with the other vehicles. If it's not absolutely required, don't stop or slow down in the acceleration lane.

Question 17 - Practice Test 1
(A) If you intend to turn beyond an intersection, wait until you are within the intersection to signal (drivers in the intersection may pull into your

path). Another car may believe you want to turn at the intersection if you signal before entering the intersection.

Question 18 - Practice Test 1
(B) If the street is too narrow to make a U-turn, you can turn around by making a three-point turn, unless it is prohibited.

Question 19 - Practice Test 1
(A) A motorcycle, like other motor vehicles, requires the entire lane width to drive safely. Even if the road is wide and the motorcycle is riding to one side, never drive alongside a motorcycle in the same lane.

Question 20 - Practice Test 1
(D) Do not attempt to swerve back onto the pavement if your vehicle's wheels have drifted onto the shoulder of the road. This may cause the vehicle to become unbalanced. Instead, slow down and stay on the shoulder, then gently, return to the road.

Question 21 - Practice Test 1
(B) Apply the brakes carefully while stopping on packed snow or ice. Braking hard on a car without anti-lock brakes (ABS) might lock the wheels and cause a skid. Pump the brakes instead. Begin by slamming on the brakes. If your wheels freeze up, let go of the brakes to get them moving again, then squeeze them down again. Continue pumping until the vehicle comes to a halt. Note: If your vehicle has anti-lock brakes, do not attempt this. ABS will pump the brakes on its own to keep the wheels from locking, allowing you to press the brake pedal firmly until the car comes to a complete stop. You can disengage the ABS by pumping the brakes.

Question 22 - Practice Test 1
(C) If you wish to make a turn, make sure other vehicles are aware of your intentions. Continue to give signals until you're ready to make the actual turn. Hand and arm extended outward is the proper hand signal for a left turn.

Question 23 - Practice Test 1
(A) Defensive driving, according to the National Safety Council, is 'driving to save lives, time and money, regardless of the conditions around you or the conduct of others'. Defensive driving is anticipating potentially, harmful scenarios, such as road conditions and other people's mistakes and devising a strategy for dealing with them. To be a defensive driver, you must be aware of what is going on around you. You must keep your eyes on the road ahead, to the sides and behind you. You owe it to yourself to learn how to drive defensively.

Question 24 - Practice Test 1
(D) Parking places for people with impairments are marked with blue pavement markings.

Question 25 - Practice Test 1
(B) If you are stopped at an intersection and another vehicle is approaching from behind at high

speed, you should move slightly forward (but not into the intersection) to give the approaching vehicle more room to stop.

Question 26 - Practice Test 1
(C) If at all feasible, park in a designated space. If you have to park on the road, try to park as far away from the traffic as possible. If a curb exists, park as close to it as possible.

Question 27 - Practice Test 1
(B) If your vehicle's turn signals have failed, you must employ hand and arm signals. The hand and arm are bent at 90 degrees and pointing upward to signify a right turn. The hand and arm are stretched leftward to indicate a left turn. The hand and arm are bent at 90 degrees and pointing downward to slow or stop.

Question 28 - Practice Test 1
(A) Airbags are dangerous for small children. Children under the age of 12 should never ride in the front seat of an airbag-equipped vehicle unless the passenger airbag is first deactivated.

Question 29 - Practice Test 1
(D) If you are one of the first people to arrive at a collision scene, the first thing you should do is pull your vehicle off the road. Then, turn off the ignition of any vehicles involved in the accident. If there is no danger of fire, do not move injured people. Notify emergency personnel and avoid standing in traffic lanes.

Inquire of those who have stopped to warn oncoming traffic.

Question 30 - Practice Test 1
(B) High-speed traffic is handled securely on freeways and interstate routes. When approaching or departing a motorway, do not cross a solid line.

Question 31 - Practice Test 1
(D) When three or more lanes are traveling in the same direction, the center lanes usually provide the smoothest traffic flow. Drivers that want to travel quicker or pass should use the left lane. The right lane should be used by slower cars and those exiting the highway.

Question 32 - Practice Test 1
(A) When a vehicle turns, the back wheels travel a lesser distance than the front wheels. The larger the difference, the longer the vehicle is. Before turning, a tractor-trailer may swing out. Don't try to pass a tractor-trailer on the right if you notice it moving left, the truck may be preparing to turn right. Examine the turn signals.

Question 33 - Practice Test 1
(C) Car and motorcycle collisions are most likely to occur at intersections. The automobile driver, in most cases, fails to detect the motorcycle and turns across its path.

Question 34 - Practice Test 1
(B) Crosswalk lines are two white or longitudinal lines that indicate where

pedestrians may walk. Do not use your vehicle to obstruct a crosswalk. Always yield to pedestrians in crosswalks, whether marked or unmarked.

Question 35 - Practice Test 1
(B) In highway and street maintenance zones, flag persons (flaggers) are frequently stationed to safely stop, delay or guide traffic through these areas. Flaggers wear orange vests, shirts or jackets and direct traffic through work zones with red or orange flags or STOP/SLOW paddles.

Question 36 - Practice Test 1
(B) Even if there are alternative lanes available, you must not pass a vehicle ahead of you that has stopped for a pedestrian. Pedestrians are frequently exposed to this danger. Instead, come to a complete stop and wait for the pedestrian to cross at least half of the road.

Question 37 - Practice Test 1
(C) When slowing or stopping, you must either use the brake-operated signal lights or a hand signal to alert the driver behind you.

Question 38 - Practice Test 1
(C) If you begin to skid, be calm, take your foot off the throttle, gently slow your vehicle down and carefully steer in the direction you want the front of your vehicle to go. In other words, if your vehicle's rear end skids left, steer left. if your vehicle's rear end skids right, steer right.

Avoid braking, particularly if your vehicle has an antilock braking system (ABS). The vehicle may overshoot and begin to slide in the opposite direction. To avoid this, turn your vehicle in the opposite direction, as soon as it begins to straighten out. This technique, known as 'driving into the skid', will align the back and front of your car.

Question 39 - Practice Test 1
(B) An intersection is a road junction at which two or more roads cross or merge. There are three types of intersections: controlled, uncontrolled and blind. An interchange is a road junction where two or more roads cross over each other (at different levels) so that traffic flow is not impeded. There are interchanges such as diamond, cloverleaf and stack.

Question 40 - Practice Test 1
(A) Make sure to keep the steering wheel straight while you tilt your head to look for blind areas. The natural propensity for people is to turn their arms in the same direction as their heads.

PRACTICE TEST 2

Question 1 - Practice Test 2

(C) On a roadway, the left lane is used for passing. If a car wishes to pass you, move to the right as safely as possible. Do not accelerate until the other vehicle has passed you.

Question 2 - Practice Test 2

(C) Warning signs inform you to probable hazards ahead. Slow down and keep an eye out for any additional signs or signals that may appear.

Question 3 - Practice Test 2

(D) When the street is too small for a U-turn, you can turn around with a three-point turn. A three-point turn is only legal if the roadway is narrow, there is good sight, traffic is light, and the turn is permitted.

Question 4 - Practice Test 2

(B) When passing a large vehicle, such as a truck, wait until you can see its headlights in your rear-view mirror before merging back in front of it. (Some experts advise waiting until you can see the complete front of the vehicle in your rearview mirror.) Stopping distances are long for large trucks. If you merge back in front of a huge car and then suddenly slow down or halt for any reason, you may be rear-ended by the large vehicle.

Question 5 - Practice Test 2

(B) A green light indicates that you may go into the junction after yielding to pedestrians and cars already present.

Question 6 - Practice Test 2

(D) Driving in the center of your lane is the safest option. Maintain as much space as possible between your vehicle and the vehicles on both sides.

Question 7 - Practice Test 2

(D) When there are no other vehicles nearby, use high beams. High beams can see twice as far as low beams. Use high beams when driving on unknown routes, in construction zones, or when there may be people on the road. In fog, rain, or snow, however, use low beams. Light from high beams reflects off of such precipitation, causing glare.

Question 8 - Practice Test 2

(A) The expressway's outer perimeter in each direction is designated with a solid white line. Following that comes the shoulder, which should only be used in an emergency. Never drive or pass on the shoulder of the road.

Question 9 - Practice Test 2

(B) If you observe solid white line separating traffic lanes, it implies you should stay in your lane until an emergency necessitates you to change lanes.

Question 10 - Practice Test 2

(C) High lights are reflected by rain, fog, and falling snow. This makes it even more difficult to see where you're going. Keep your vehicle's headlights on low beam for enhanced visibility during these weather conditions.

Question 11 - Practice Test 2

(D) You must keep a safe distance. Wait until you can see the headlights of the passed vehicle in your rear-view mirror before attempting to return to your previous lane. Turn on your turn signal, check your blind areas, and then return to your previous lane.

Question 12 - Practice Test 2

(B) The United States Drug Enforcement Administration (DEA) and the United States Food and Drug Administration (FDA) keep a list of controlled dangerous substances (CDSs). These are substances that are restricted in their manufacture, importation, possession, usage, and distribution. Substances classified as Schedule I have a significant potential for misuse and no recognized medicinal use in the United States. As an example, consider heroin.

Question 13 - Practice Test 2

(B) Not wearing a seat belt in a crash is even more harmful. If you wear your seat belt, you are considerably more likely to be conscious and unharmed, and so able to escape if you become stuck. Your seat belt also aids in keeping you behind the wheel regardless of what happens. If you slide out from behind the wheel, you will lose control of your vehicle.

Question 14 - Practice Test 2

(A) Your stopping distance is equal to the sum of your response and braking distances. If you are driving quickly, weary, or your vehicle has faulty brakes, you will need to stop your vehicle for a longer distance.

Question 15 - Practice Test 2

(B) Rumble strips are indentation features that are erected on a paved roadway shoulder near the travel lane, on a two-lane roadway along the center line, or in traffic lanes approaching a stop sign or signal. Rumble strips use vibration and sound to inform fatigued or inattentive drivers that their cars have left the travel lane or are approaching a stop sign.

Question 16 - Practice Test 2

(C) Mobile devices such as electronic message signs and flashing arrow panels are used on some roadways to provide early warning of work zones or unusual conditions at or near work zones.

Question 17 - Practice Test 2

(A) If your vehicle is hit from the side, your body will appear to be tossed to that side — relative to the car, that is. The side of the car that was hit is actually being pushed toward you in relation to the ground.

Question 18 - Practice Test 2

(C) When exiting a high-speed, two-lane highway, try not to slow down abruptly or you may get rear-ended by the vehicle ahead of you. Use your turn signals to communicate your intentions to other vehicles. Use your brakes to slow down swiftly but safely.

Question 19 - Practice Test 2

(C) If an animal suddenly runs in front of your vehicle, try to keep the vehicle under control to avoid a collision. Slow down gradually. You should not attempt to drive around the animal. Stay in your car. Do not stop to watch the animal or chase it off the road. Allow the animal lots of space and allow it to meander off the road.

Question 20 - Practice Test 2

(B) If you brake forcefully at high speed, the force of the brakes may exceed the friction force of the tires on the road surface. No matter which way the steering wheel is cranked, the wheels will lock and the vehicle will skid. Take your foot off the brake to free the wheels and you'll be able to recover from the skid. Then, as the car begins to straighten out, straighten the front wheels. Slow the vehicle down gradually until you are at a safe pace to continue driving.

Question 21 - Practice Test 2

(C) If one of your visitors is involved in a drunk-driving accident after leaving your premises, you could face a lawsuit. Don't let any of your guests drive if they've had too much to drink. Instead, call a taxi for them or (if it's safe) invite them to remain with you until they sober up.

Question 22 - Practice Test 2

(C) If your rear wheels begin to skid, remain calm, take your foot off the gas, and slowly guide your vehicle in the direction you want it to travel. This technique, known as "steering into the skid," will bring your vehicle's rear end into level with the front. Then, if your car has anti-lock brakes, you can softly brake (if it does) or gently pump the brake pedal (if it does not) to slow down even further.

Question 23 - Practice Test 2

(A) When turning left at a controlled junction, you must yield to oncoming traffic and stop for pedestrians at a crosswalk.

Question 24 - Practice Test 2

(A) At a junction, a stop line is a solid white line painted across the approach lane. Before the crosswalk, there is a stop line. If you are required to stop by a stop sign or traffic light, you must halt before the stop line. In most cities, the stop line is around four feet before the crossing.

Question 25 - Practice Test 2

(B) When turning left from a two-way street onto a one-way street, start with your left wheel as close to the yellow dividing line as possible.

Question 26 - Practice Test 2

(D) When driving in city traffic, attempt to glance at least one block ahead. In the city, 10 seconds equals approximately one block.

Question 27 - Practice Test 2

(C) Check for traffic behind and to the side of your vehicle before changing lanes. Check to see if there are any vehicles in the lane you want to enter.

Question 28 - Practice Test 2

(C) Unless your car has antilock brakes, if your brakes fail, push the brake pedal (ABS). Pumping may restore enough brake fluid pressure to slow or stop your vehicle temporarily. If your vehicle has ABS, simply depress the brake pedal hard and see whether you begin to slow down. Shift down into a lower gear. This will use the engine's braking power to slow your vehicle. Apply the parking or emergency brake gradually but be prepared to let go if you begin to slide. Rub against something as a final option to slow you down. Attempt to sideswipe the guard rail, scrape your tires against a curb, or drive onto grass. Allowing a head-on collision is never a good idea. Accidents involving a head-on collision are frequently fatal.

Question 29 - Practice Test 2

(A) The only form of sign that is pennant shaped is the No Passing Zone sign. It marks the beginning of a no-passing zone for any vehicles traveling in your direction. This sign can be found on the left side of the road.

Question 30 - Practice Test 2

(A) Because mopeds and motorcycles are smaller than most other vehicles, they are more difficult to see. A moped or motorcycle can easily be missed if it is hidden in your blind spot.

Question 31 - Practice Test 2

(C) When changing lanes, make sure there are no vehicles in your blind spots by looking over your shoulder in the direction you intend to move. These areas are not visible in your mirrors.

Question 32 - Practice Test 2

(C) If you intend to turn beyond an intersection, the signal just after passing through it. If you signal too early, another car may mistakenly believe you are turning at the intersection.

Question 33 - Practice Test 2

(D) Slower speeds are required in bad weather. You should keep a greater distance from other vehicles. Rain, snow, and ice reduce your ability to see ahead and increase the amount of time it takes to stop your vehicle. Increase your following distance and apply your brakes sooner and more gently than usual in such conditions.

Question 34 - Practice Test 2

(B) On ice, it is best to slow to a crawl. If chains are required for increased traction, keep in mind that even chains and snow tires might slip on ice and packed snow.

Question 35 - Practice Test 2

(A) DON'T PANIC if you have a sudden tire blowout. Also, don't slam on the brakes too hard or you'll lock the wheels and lose control. Only use the brakes softly if absolutely essential and safe to do so. Take a tight grip on the steering wheel and release your foot from the pedal to allow your car to come to a complete halt. Do not move to the road's shoulder until you have slowed significantly. If the blowout has led your vehicle to swerve onto the shoulder, do not attempt to return to the pavement right away. Allow the vehicle to come to a complete stop first.

Question 36 - Practice Test 2

(B) If the green arrow turns yellow, it indicates that a red arrow, steady red light, or steady green light is about to appear. If you're already in the junction, don't obstruct it. Complete your maneuver and quickly clear the junction.

Question 37 - Practice Test 2

(B) Don't try to cross the tracks at a railroad crossing until you can do so without stopping. If you shift gears while crossing the tracks, your vehicle may stall.

Question 38 - Practice Test 2

(D) If your vehicle's turn signals fail, use hand signals until they can be repaired. However, keep in mind that hand signals may not be visible in the dark.

Question 39 - Practice Test 2

(B) When making a U-turn, you must give pedestrians and oncoming cars the right-of-way. If other cars approaching from either direction cannot see you, do not make a U-turn on a curve or near the top of a hill.

Question 40 - Practice Test 2

(C) On streets and highways, diagonal yellow striping indicates a narrow road or an impending obstruction.

ROAD SIGNS

Question 1 - Road Signals Full
(A) This is a forewarning sign that may be placed ahead of the railroad crossing. Vehicles must slow down, look, listen and be prepared to come to a complete stop at the crossing ahead.

Question 2 - Road Signs
(A) Sequential arrow panels can be used in work zones 24 hours a day, seven days a week. This one indicates that the lane ahead is closed and that you should take the lane to your left.

Question 3 - Road Signs
(B) Route marker signs indicate the type of road you're on as well as the specific road you're on. Highway marker signs are typically shield-shaped and Interstate shield signs are colored red, white and blue. This sign denotes that you are on Interstate Highway 22. (I-22 for short). I-22 connects Mississippi's I-269 to Alabama's I-65.

Question 4 - Road Signs
(C) These are lane guidance signs. Vehicles on the left must turn left, while vehicles on the right may either continue straight or turn right.

Question 5 - Road Signs
(B) Traffic moving in opposite directions is separated by yellow lines. On two-way streets, there will be either a double solid yellow line or a solid yellow line next to a broken yellow line.

Question 6 - Road Signs
(C) This sign indicates that the divided highway is coming to an end. The road will be converted to a two-way street. Keep to the right and keep an eye out for oncoming traffic.

Question 7 - Road Signs
(B) This sign is typically displayed at an intersection with a combination of signals, including a green arrow pointing left. When the green arrow is illuminated, you may make a protected left turn. Oncoming traffic will be stopped at a red light. This sign indicates that if the green arrow disappears and a steady green light appears, you may still make a left turn, but you must now yield to oncoming traffic, before turning.

Question 8 - Road Signs
(D) This sign indicates that traffic in the right lane must turn right, while traffic in the second lane may either continue straight or turn right.

Question 9 - Road Signs
(B) A disabled crossing is indicated by the sign ahead. Slow down and take your time.

Question 10 - Road Signs
(D) This is a red flag. Bicyclists and pedestrians frequently cross the road in the vicinity of the sign. You must drive cautiously and be prepared to stop.

Question 11 - Road Signs
(B) This railroad crossing signal features a bell and flashing red

lights to alert drivers that a train is approaching. When the bell rings and the lights flash, come to a halt.

Question 12 - Road Signs
(A) When the road ahead is clear, this image indicates that passing on the left is permitted. Due to oncoming traffic, overtaking and passing should be done with caution.

Question 13 - Road Signs
(D) This sign indicates that a rest area is available on the right.

Question 14 - Road Signs
(C) This is a warning sign indicating the presence of a playground ahead.

Question 15 - Road Signs
(A) This sign denotes a service. It denotes a rest stop one mile ahead.

Question 16 - Road Signs
(A) This sign warns drivers that a nearby side road crosses a railroad track. When turning onto the side road, proceed with caution.

Question 17 - Road Signs
(C) This sign indicates that you are not permitted to park in a handicap zone unless you have the necessary permit.

Question 18 - Road Signs
(C) A vehicle with a reflective triangular orange emblem on the rear identifies it as a low-speed or slow-moving vehicle, which is typically defined as a motor vehicle with a top speed of no more than 25 mph. Farm vehicles and road maintenance vehicles are examples of slow-moving vehicles. Slow down and proceed with caution if you come across one of these vehicles.

Question 19 - Road Signs
(B) Blue-and-white signs direct you to services such as gas stations, fast-food restaurants, motels and hospitals. The sign in picture B indicates that there is a hospital ahead.

Question 20 - Road Signs
(C) The larger sign alerts you to the impending arrival of a speed zone. The speed limit is indicated by the smaller sign. The speed limit will be reduced to 45 mph ahead in this case. Prepare to slow down so that you don't go over the speed limit.

Question 21 - Road Signs
(A) Vertical rectangular signs typically provide instructions or inform you of traffic laws. Motorists, pedestrians and cyclists are given instructions by such regulatory signs.

Question 22 - Road Signs
(C) This sign indicates that the road ahead curves in the direction indicated by the arrow.

Question 23 - Road Signs
(B) This sign indicates a bicycle crossing. This sign forewarns you that a bikeway will cross the road ahead.

Question 24 - Road Signs

(C) If you see this sign while driving in the left lane, turn left at the next intersection.

Question 25 - Road Signs

(D) This sign indicates that there will be a double curve ahead. The road ahead bends to the right, then to the left. (A winding road sign would be posted instead if there was a triple curve ahead.) Slow down, stay to the right and do not pass.

Question 26 - Road Signs

(D) Pedestrian signals are only used to direct pedestrian traffic. This pedestrian signal indicates that pedestrians may enter the crosswalk to cross the road. (Older signals displayed the word 'WALK' instead.) A signal with an upraised hand warns pedestrians not to enter the crosswalk. (Older signals displayed the words 'DO NOT WALK' instead.)

Question 27 - Road Signs

(A) This is a navigational sign. This sign indicates the presence of a hospital ahead.

Question 28 - Road Signs

(D) You must follow the broken yellow centerline to the right. When it is safe to do so, you may cross this line, to pass another vehicle or turn.

Question 29 - Road Signs

(A) This sign indicates an exit number. This is the number assigned to a highway exit at a junction. If an interchange has more than one exit, a letter may be added to indicate which exit it is: 117A, 117B and so on.

Question 30 - Road Signs

(A) This is a service sign directing you to a gas station.

Question 31 - Road Signs

(B) This sign warns that the road ahead will be divided into a divided highway. A divider, also known as a median, will be used to separate opposing lanes. Continue to the right.

Question 32 - Road Signs

(A) Travelers can get important information from dynamic message signs. Messages can be changed to reflect current weather conditions, route traffic, construction schedules, incidents and so on.

Question 33 - Road Signs

(B) If you see this sign, it means you're driving in the wrong direction. Make a U-turn.

Question 34 - Road Signs

(D) This sign indicates that the maximum nighttime speed limit is 45 mph.

Question 35 - Road Signs

(A) This is a warning sign for emergency vehicles. It denotes that emergency vehicles from fire stations or other emergency facilities may enter the roadway. When an emergency vehicle approaches from any direction, you must yield to it if it is sounding a siren, blowing an air horn or flashing lights.

Question 36 - Road Signs

(D) This sign may be found at the end of some T-intersections. It means that you must yield the right of way or come to a complete stop, before turning right or left onto the through road.

Question 37 - Road Signs

(C) The middle lane is a two-way left-turn lane, also known as a shared center turning lane, according to the sign and pavement markings. Vehicles coming from either direction may enter this lane only to turn left. This lane must not be used for through traffic at any time.

Question 38 - Road Signs

(C) This sign indicates that U-turns are not permitted in this area.

Question 39 - Road Signs

(B) This sign denotes a T-junction. This sign indicates that the road you're on is about to come to an end. Prepare to make a right or left turn. Yield to oncoming traffic.

Question 40 - Road Signs

(C) At a roundabout, this is a speed advisory sign. In the roundabout, the speed limit is 15 mph.

Question 41 - Road Signs

(D) This is a traffic control sign. This sign indicates that traffic must only make a left turn.

Question 42 - Road Signs

(A) The arrow represents a turn to the right. A red slash inside a red circle, on the other hand, means 'no'. This regulatory sign forbids drivers from turning right. This sign is usually found on the right side of the road or above a travel lane.

Question 43 - Road Signs

(B) This sign denotes a service. It indicates that telephone service is available and within proximity.

Question 44 - Road Signs

(B) This sign is located next to a route marker sign. It means you'll have to turn right soon to enter or continue on that route.

Question 45 - Road Signs

(B) This sign indicates the maximum safe speed for entering or exiting an expressway. Slow down to the indicated speed (in this case, 30 mph).

(B) Question 46 - Road Signs

A two-lane, two-way road may have a single broken (dashed) yellow line. If it is safe to do so, vehicles on either side may pass.

Question 47 - Road Signs

(C) This regulatory sign indicates a complete halt. At a stop sign, you must come to a complete stop before the stop line, crosswalk or intersection, whichever comes first. After that, yield to pedestrians and other vehicles and proceed only when the intersection is clear. You must come to a complete stop near the sign and yield the right-of-way to other vehicles.

Question 48 - Road Signs
(D) Lane use control signs are rectangular, black-and-white signs that indicate, whether or not, turning is required from specified lanes at an intersection. You must only drive in the direction indicated for your traffic lane.

Question 49 - Road Signs
(B) This sign indicates the presence of a four-way intersection ahead. Cross-traffic entering the roadway should be avoided by drivers.

Question 50 - Road Signs
(A) No is represented by a red circle with a diagonal red slash. The red slash across the truck denotes that trucks are not permitted on this road. Truck drivers must seek alternate routes.

Question 51 - Road Signs
(A) This sign denotes a railroad crossing with low ground clearance. The railroad crossing is elevated to the point where a vehicle with a long wheelbase or low ground clearance can become stuck on the tracks. This type of railroad crossing should not be a problem for a car driver unless he or she is towing a trailer or driving a motorhome with low ground clearance.

Question 52 - Road Signs
(B) If there is a broken or dashed line (white or yellow) next to your lane, you may pass if it is safe to do so.

Question 53 - Road Signs
(C) A stop sign is a white-on-red eight-sided sign that indicates that other traffic has the right-of-way. Before proceeding, you must always come to a complete stop and yield to oncoming traffic.

Question 54 - Road Signs
(D) Work zone signs alert motorists to unusual or potentially hazardous conditions on or near the traveled route. The letters or symbols on these signs are black on an orange background. Slow down and pay close attention if you see these signs.

Question 55 - Road Signs
(A) Sequencing or large flashing Arrow panels can be used in work zones both during the day and at night, to direct drivers into specific traffic lanes and to notify them that a portion of the road or street ahead is closed.

Question 56 - Road Signs
(A) The arrow's shape indicates that you're about to enter a winding road. There are at least three curves on a winding road. Slow down and take your time.

Question 57 - Road Signs
(C) When the road surface is wet, it becomes slick. This sign is frequently found near bridges and overpasses.

Question 58 - Road Signs

(B) This is a sign for a freeway interchange. This sign alerts you to the fact that you are approaching an interchange.

Question 59 - Road Signs
(C) This sign indicates that you are approaching an overpass, with a clearance of 13 feet 6 inches from the roadway surface to the overpass.

Question 60 - Road Signs
(D) This sign indicates that you are not permitted to park on the left side of the sign at any time.

Question 61 - Road Signs
(A) This is a crossing sign for animals. The animal depicted on the sign (in this case, a deer) is common in this area. Keep an eye out for these animals crossing the road, especially at dawn and dusk. Herds of deer, elk and other wildlife travel in groups. If you see one, keep an eye out for more. A collision with a large animal has the potential to kill the animal, damage your vehicle and even injure a passenger in your vehicle.

Question 62 - Road Signs
(C) When there are children present, this sign warns drivers not to exceed the posted speed limit in a school zone or school crossing. The maximum permissible speed, in this case, is 15 mph.

Question 63 - Road Signs
(B) This is a sign indicating a service. It is recommended that drivers use lodging facilities if necessary.

Question 64 - Road Signs
(A) This white diamond sign indicates that the road is reserved for high-occupancy vehicles (HOVs) from Monday to Friday, at the times specified.

Question 65 - Road Signs
(D) A stop sign accompanied by this sign at an intersection indicates that the intersection is a four-way stop. Each approaching roadway is marked with a stop sign and a '4-Way' sign.

Question 66 - Road Signs
(B) This sign alerts you to the fact that you are about to approach a T-intersection from the terminating roadway. You must turn left or right at the T-intersection after yielding the right-of-way to through traffic if necessary.

Question 67 - Road Signs
(A) This sign directs you to turn right onto Route 47 and head north.

Question 68 - Road Signs
(B) This is a warning sign indicating that you are approaching an airport.

Question 69 - Road Signs
(A) This sign indicates a side road ahead. Keep an eye out for vehicles approaching from that direction.

Question 70 - Road Signs
(B) This sign indicates a sharp left turn. Slow down (to the

recommended speed of 25 mph, in this case), keep right as you turn and do not pass.

Question 71 - Road Signs

(D) A speed limit sign indicates the maximum legal speed permitted on the expressway under ideal driving conditions.

Question 72 - Road Signs

(D) The school zone sign is pentagonal in shape (five sides) and has a yellow or yellow-green background.

Question 73 - Road Signs

(C) This sign warns of a road closure ahead, but there is an alternate route in 1,000 feet.

Question 74 - Road Signs

(B) This sign indicates that there will be a hiccup in the road ahead. To avoid losing control, slow down.

Question 75 - Road Signs

(B) Pedestrian signals are only used to direct pedestrian traffic. This signal with an upraised hand informs pedestrians that they are not permitted to enter the crosswalk to cross the roadway. (Older signals displayed the words 'DO NOT WALK' instead.) Pedestrians may enter the crosswalk if they see a signal depicting a person walking. (Older signals displayed the word 'WALK' instead.)

Question 76 - Road Signs

(A) Yellow lines separate traffic lanes traveling in opposite

directions. Except when turning left, do not cross a solid yellow line.

Question 77 - Road Signs

(D) This work zone sign indicates that there will be a flagger (flag person) ahead. Flaggers are frequently found in highway or street construction zones. They wear orange vests, shirts or jackets and use red flags or STOP/SLOW paddles to direct traffic through these areas safely. You must obey the flagger's instructions.

Question 78 - Road Signs

(A) If you see this sign while driving on the main road, be prepared for other cars and trucks to enter your lane.

Question 79 - Road Signs

(A) This is a warning sign indicating the presence of a narrow bridge ahead. The bridge is wide enough for two lanes of traffic, but there is very little clearance.

Question 80 - Road Signs

(B) This type of warning sign alerts drivers ahead of a reduction in the number of lanes. This sign indicates that the right lane is coming to an end ahead. Drivers in the right lane are required to merge to the left. Drivers in the left lane should give way to vehicles in the right lane so that they can merge smoothly.

Question 81 - Road Signs

(C) Consider a flashing red light to be a stop sign. To put it another way, come to a complete stop and then yield the right-of-way before proceeding.

Question 82 - Road Signs
(B) White lines separate traffic lanes moving in the same direction. You must drive between these lane markings.

Question 83 - Road Signs
(C) This sign indicates that workers are performing road maintenance. Slow down, be cautious and obey all signs and instructions. If possible, move into a lane that is further away from the workers.

Question 84 - Road Signs
(A) The majority of warning signs are diamond-shaped and have a yellow background. This sign alerts you to the impending arrival of a stop sign. Prepare to come to a halt and yield. You must come to a complete stop before any stop line or crosswalk, painted on the pavement.

Question 85 - Road Signs
(C) This pentagonal (five-sided) sign indicates that you are approaching a school zone.

Question 86 - Road Signs
(D) A red circle and slash on a prohibitory sign, means 'no'. This sign indicates that left turns are not permitted in this area.

Question 87 - Road Signs
(B) This sign indicates an exit number. These signs direct you to bike paths, parking lots, mile markers and specific exits. You can see how far you are from the exit you want to take, by entering the milepost number and the exit number.

Question 88 - Road Signs
(A) This symbol denotes a soft shoulder. The dirt on the roadside is soft. Except in an emergency, never leave the pavement.

Question 89 - Road Signs
(A) This sign indicates the presence of a traffic island or divider ahead. Keep to the left of this stumbling block.

Question 90 - Road Signs
(A) A red slash within a red circle denotes 'no'. This sign indicates that driving on the railroad tracks is prohibited

Question 91 - Road Signs
(D) A red slash within a red circle denotes 'no'. Pedestrians are not permitted to cross here, according to this regulatory sign.

Question 92 - Road Signs
(A) This is a warning sign indicating a two-way street.

Question 93 - Road Signs
(A) This sign denotes a bicycle lane, which is intended for bicyclists. Cars and trucks should not normally use this lane. Cars and trucks may, however, travel in this lane for a short distance when preparing to

turn at the next intersection in many (but not all) states.

Question 94 - Road Signs
(A) This symbol denotes a Y-intersection. The road ahead divides into two directions. Be prepared to turn in one direction or the other, if traffic crosses your path.

Question 95 - Road Signs
(D) Guide signs inform drivers about the type of road they are on, upcoming highway entrances and exits and distances to various destinations. Shield-shaped guide signs are commonly used to identify U.S. Routes and interstate highways. This sign informs you that you are on Interstate 95 (I-95), which runs from Maine to Florida.

Question 96 - Road Signs
(C) The International Symbol of Access for Disabled People is featured on this sign. This means that these parking spaces are only available to people who have disabled parking permits. You must obtain a disabled parking placard or disabled license plates from your state, to park in these spaces.

Question 97 - Road Signs
(B) This sign warns drivers to be on the lookout for cattle crossing the road.

Question 98 - Road Signs
(C) In North America, raising one's hand with the thumb indicates that one wishes to hitch a ride. A red slash within a red circle denotes 'no'.

This sign indicates that hitchhiking is prohibited on this stretch of road. Please do not pick up hitchhikers here.

Question 99 - Road Signs
(D) This is a route marker sign for the United States. A route marker sign's shape and color indicate the type of road you're on. Shield-shaped signs are commonly used to identify U.S. Routes and interstate highways. This sign indicates that you are on US Highway 40. The United States Routes are a network of roads and highways that were built decades before the Interstate Highway System. US Route 40 was built in 1926 and currently connects Silver Summit, UT to Atlantic City, NJ.

Question 100 - Road Signs
(C) This symbol indicates the presence of a pedestrian crosswalk ahead. Pedestrians must be given the right of way by drivers.

Question 101 - Road Signs
(B) This sign indicates that all vehicles are not permitted to pass through this area (buses, trucks, passenger cars, etc.).

Question 102 - Road Signs
(C) A red slash within a red circle denotes 'no'. Bicycles are not permitted on this route, as indicated by this prohibitory sign.

Question 103 - Road Signs
(D) This is an object marker sign, which is used to alert drivers to

objects in the road or very close to the road's edge. The stripes point down the road, toward the safe side. This sign indicates that you should continue to the right to pass the object.

Question 104 - Road Signs
(B) Parking is prohibited between 8:30 a.m. and 5:30 p.m., according to this sign.

Question 105 - Road Signs
(A) The road shoulder is much lower than the road surface, as indicated by this sign.

Question 106 - Road Signs
(D) Most states in the United States impose additional penalties for certain traffic violations in work zones under certain conditions, though the conditions and additional penalties vary by state. This sign warns drivers that fines for exceeding the posted speed limit in work zones have been doubled.

Question 107 - Road Signs
(B) This sign warns drivers that there will be a railroad crossing ahead. Drivers must exercise extreme caution.

Question 108 - Road Signs
(A) This sign indicates that there is a speed limit ahead. This is a zone where the speed limit has been reduced. Prepare to slow down so you don't go over the speed limit.

Question 109 - Road Signs
(A) This sign indicates that you may not drive slower than 40 mph under normal traffic, weather and road conditions. These minimum speed limits are in place to improve traffic flow and safety. However, if driving conditions are hazardous, you may drive at a slower speed than the posted minimum.

Question 110 - Road Signs
(A) Lane-use control signals are special overhead signals that allow or disallow the use of specific streets or highway lanes. A continuous red X over a lane indicates that you must not drive in that lane.

Question 111 - Road Signs
(D) This sign indicates that trucks are about to enter or cross the road ahead. Slow down and keep an eye out for trucks.

Question 112 - Road Signs
(A) This sign forewarns of a steep descent ahead. Before you begin the descent, inspect your brakes. Even if your vehicle has an automatic transmission, use low gear to reduce brake wear.

Question 113 - Road Signs
(A) This sign indicates that you are approaching the intersection of your road and U.S. Route 22. The United States Routes are a network of roads and highways that were built decades before the Interstate Highway System. One of the oldest is U.S. Route 22, which connects

Cincinnati, Ohio and Newark, New Jersey.

Question 114 - Road Signs
(D) This sign indicates that the vertical clearance on this road is 12'6". (twelve feet six inches). Vehicles taller than this should avoid using this road. Trucks in the United States can legally stand taller than 13 feet.

Question 115 - Road Signs
(A) The sign warns the driver that there will be two-way traffic ahead. Drivers must keep an eye out for traffic coming from the opposite direction.

Question 116 - Road Signs
(C) This is a stop sign. If it is safe to do so, this sign allows you to make a U-turn.

Question 117 - Road Signs
(C) This is a regulatory sign instructing you to continue straight or make a right turn.

Question 118 - Road Signs
(D) This sign indicates that you are not permitted to enter the roadway where the sign is posted.

Question 119 - Road Signs
(D) A diamond-shaped marking indicates that a lane is reserved for specific purposes or vehicles. During rush hour, the lanes are usually reserved for buses or carpool vehicles.

Question 120 - Road Signs

(B) This is a sign with a directional arrow.

Question 121 - Road Signs
(D) This sign indicates that there will be a roundabout ahead. A roundabout is a circular intersection with traffic flowing counterclockwise around a central island. In the roundabout, slow down and prepare to yield to traffic.

Question 122 - Road Signs
(A) This sign forewarns of an impending traffic signal. If the light is yellow or red, prepare to come to a complete stop. These signs are placed on highways with higher speed limits or where your view of the traffic signal ahead may be obstructed.

Question 123 - Road Signs
(C) This warning sign alerts drivers to the possibility of farm equipment crossing the road. Prepare to slow down for slow-moving machinery.

Question 124 - Road Signs
(B) This sign indicates that the road ahead will take a sharp right turn. Slow down and proceed with caution.

Question 125 - Road Signs
(C) At freeway exits and entrance ramps, signs like this one, provide advisory speeds. They display the maximum safe speed to drive at in ideal weather conditions.

Question 126 - Road Signs
(C) This sign indicates that you are not permitted to turn on a red light. To turn right, you must first wait for a green arrow or green light.

Question 127 - Road Signs
(B) Mileposts are spaced at regular intervals so that drivers are always aware of them. They are installed along the road's edge to provide drivers with information about their location on the highway for navigation and emergency purposes. The distance in miles to the state line or the end of the road is usually indicated by the number on the milepost.

Question 128 - Road Signs
(B) Most public crossings have railroad flashing light signals and crossbuck signs. These signs must be handled in the same manner as a yield sign.

Question 129 - Road Signs
(A) This sign is a nighttime reflector that indicates the location of the road.

Question 130 - Road Signs
(C) Passing is permitted when it can be done safely, as indicated by broken white lines.

Question 131 - Road Signs
(B) During road closures or construction, this sign indicates alternate routes. Pay attention to these cues.

Question 132 - Road Signs
(D) Two lanes traveling in the same direction are separated by a white line. You may cross a broken line to pass or change lanes. You should usually stay in your lane if it's a straight line.

Question 133 - Road Signs
(D) This sign regulates traffic and instructs drivers whether to turn left or straight.

Question 134 - Road Signs
(C) A red slash within a red circle denotes 'no'. This regulatory sign reads 'No Parking'. It is not permitted to park at the sign.

Question 135 - Road Signs
(B) This sign indicates that you must proceed straight. You are unable to turn here.

Question 136 - Road Signs
(C) The center lane is designated for left turns (or U-turns when permitted) and can be used by vehicles traveling in either direction. On the pavement, left-turn arrows for one-way traffic alternate with left-turn arrows for the opposite direction. These lanes are denoted by solid and broken (dashed) yellow lines on each side.

Question 137 - Road Signs
(B) This is a yield sign, which is the only type of sign that has a downward-pointing triangle shape. When you come to a yield sign, you must slow down and yield to oncoming traffic and pedestrians before proceeding. You may need to

stop for them as well, so be prepared.

Question 138 - Road Signs

(B) This out-of-the-ordinary lane control sign indicates that all vehicles in this lane must perform a U-turn. This sign could be accompanied by an equally unusual traffic signal, with lighted U-turn arrows indicating when vehicles can make U-turns.

Question 139 - Road Signs

(C) The road ahead abruptly changes direction. Drivers must reduce their speed to a safe level.

Question 140 - Road Signs

(B) HOV lanes are intended for vehicles that have multiple occupants, such as carpools. This sign indicates that this HOV lane is an HOV 2+ lane, which means that each vehicle must have at least two occupants. That is, there must be a driver and at least one passenger.

Question 141 - Road Signs

(D) This sign serves as a forewarning of an impending yield sign. Be prepared to slow down and yield to vehicles approaching from other directions.

Question 142 - Road Signs

(D) This sign indicates the presence of a shared, central turn lane (also known as a two-way left-turn lane) in the center of the roadway. This lane is designated for left turns (and, where permitted, U-turns) and can be used by vehicles traveling in

either direction. A solid yellow line and a broken yellow line mark the lane on each side. This lane must not be used for through traffic at any time. Use caution in this lane because vehicles traveling in the opposite direction may be using it as well.

Question 143 - Road Signs

(C) This sign indicates that there is a low spot ahead on the road. Slow down for your own comfort and control. Proceed with caution and be prepared to stop if the dip becomes flooded.

Question 144 - Road Signs

(C) This sign indicates that the speed limit is 40 miles per hour. This is the fastest you can travel in ideal conditions.

Question 145 - Road Signs

(D) This sign indicates that traffic may flow on both sides of the road.

Question 146 - Road Signs

(D) The main road will curve to the left, with a side road entering from the right, according to this sign. Take extra care when approaching this intersection. A driver preparing to enter the main road from a side road may not notice you approaching from around the curve and may pull out in front of you.

Question 147 - Road Signs

(C) This warning sign indicates that there is a right-hand curve ahead. Just below the sign, a recommended safe speed for the curve may be shown.

Question 148 - Road Signs
(B) This one-way sign warns drivers that they must only travel in the direction indicated by the arrow.

Question 149 - Road Signs
(C) If you see this sign and are traveling slower than the majority of traffic, move to the right lane so that faster traffic can pass you on the left.

Question 150 - Road Signs
(A) This is a wayfinding sign. This sign indicates that food is available

SIGNS AND SITUATIONS

Question 1 - Signs and Situations
(B) This sign warns of a traffic island or other impending hazard. It can be passed on either the left or right side.

Question 2 - Signs and Situations
(C) This sign alerts you that you are approaching an underpass with a vertical clearance of 13'6" (13 feet 6 inches). Trucks can legally be up to 14 feet tall in many Western states (and in a few Western states, even taller).

Question 3 - Signs and Situations
(D) When approaching an intersection controlled by a stop sign, you must come to a complete stop before the stop line. If there is no stop line, you must come to a complete stop before entering a marked or unmarked crosswalk. If there is no crosswalk, you must come to a complete stop before entering the intersection. Yield to oncoming traffic and pedestrians. When it is safe to do so, proceed cautiously through the intersection.

Question 4 - Signs and Situations
(A) When two vehicles arrive at an uncontrolled intersection (one without signs or signals) around the same time, the vehicle on the left must yield to the vehicle on the right. Car A must yield to Car B in this situation.

Question 5 - Signs and Situations
(C) When you can't see well or other drivers can't see you, turn on your headlights. You must use your headlights from half an hour after sunset to half an hour before sunrise, as well as whenever visibility at 500 feet is poor. In addition, unless the wipers are set to intermittent or 'mist', you must use your headlights whenever you use your windshield wipers in bad weather. Your parking lights are intended for parking only, not driving.

Question 6 - Signs and Situations
(A) This is a shared central turning lane with a two-way left turn lane. This lane is for vehicles traveling in either direction making a left turn. Use caution in this lane because vehicles traveling in the opposite direction may be using it as well. This lane should never be used to pass.

Question 7 - Signs and Situations
(A) This pentagonal (five-sided) sign forewarns of an impending school zone or school crossing. Slow down and proceed with caution as school children may be crossing the road ahead. Follow the instructions of the school crossing guards. (Please keep in mind that newer school zones and crossing signs have a fluorescent yellow-green background.)

Question 8 - Signs and Situations

(B) According to the Driver Manual, the following distance of at least two seconds behind the vehicle in front, is recommended. You should increase your following distance even more in hazardous driving conditions.

Question 9 - Signs and Situations

(D) Parking within 15 feet of a fire hydrant is illegal. (There are numerous other places where you are not permitted to park.) Look for any signs or pavement markings that prohibit or limit parking.

Question 10 - Signs and Situations

(A) This sign indicates that there will be a double curve ahead. The road ahead bends to the right, then to the left. (A winding road sign would be posted instead if there was a triple curve ahead.) Slow down, stay to the right and do not pass.

Question 11 - Signs and Situations

(A) A steady yellow traffic light indicates that the light will soon turn red. If it is safe to do so, you should try to stop. (Never try to 'beat the light' by speeding up before it turns red.) But don't come to a sudden halt and risk skidding or being rear-ended by the vehicle in front of you. If you are unable to stop safely, proceed through the intersection with caution.

Question 12 - Signs and Situations

(B) On a green signal, you can turn left after yielding to pedestrians, oncoming vehicles and vehicles already in the intersection.

Question 13 - Signs and Situations

(D) This hand signal is equivalent to the driver's vehicle's brake lights. This driver intends to slow down or come to a complete stop.

Question 14 - Signs and Situations

(A) This sign warns you that traffic from the right lane is about to merge into your lane. Adjust your speed and position to allow merging vehicles to safely merge.

Question 15 - Signs and Situations

(A) Hand signals can be used in place of your vehicle's traditional lighted turn and brake signals. This hand signal indicates a turn to the right.

Question 16 - Signs and Situations

(B) This sign indicates that the divided highway is coming to an end. The road will be converted to a two-way street. Keep to the right and keep an eye out for oncoming traffic.

Question 17 - Signs and Situations

(D) If there is a stop sign, a flashing red signal or a lowered crossing gate at a railroad crossing, you must come to a complete stop. If you must stop, you must do so within 15 to 50 feet of the nearest rail. A railroad crossing gate may not be passed through unless it is completely raised. Always keep an eye out for and listen for approaching trains. warning devices can fail.

Question 18 - Signs and Situations

(D) Before changing lanes, signal and check your mirrors. However, your vehicle has blind spots large enough to conceal another vehicle in the lane next to yours. Motorcyclists are frequently forced to avoid drivers who have failed to check their blind spots. Looking over your shoulder before changing lanes is the only way to check for blind spots. Otherwise, you may fail to notice the vehicle in front of you until it is too late.

Question 19 - Signs and Situations

(A) When two vehicles approach an all-way stop at roughly the same time, the vehicle on the left must yield to the vehicle on the right. Car A must yield to Car B in this situation.

Question 20 - Signs and Situations

(A) If you see a school bus stopped with its red lights flashing on an undivided roadway, you must stop before reaching the bus, whether it is on your side of the road or the opposite side. You must stay stopped until the stop arm retracts and the flashing red lights go out.

Question 21 - Signs and Situations

(B) You must signal continuously for at least the last 100 feet before turning. Even if you don't see any other vehicles, you must signal. The most dangerous vehicle may be one you don't notice.

Question 22 - Signs and Situations

(D) Before proceeding through a red light, you must come to a complete stop and yield to all pedestrians and approaching vehicles.

Question 23 - Signs and Situations

(C) When you come across an emergency vehicle, sanitation vehicle, utility vehicle or wrecker that is stopped with its flashing lights on, you must move into a non-adjacent lane if possible, leaving at least one vacant lane between you and the vehicle. If this is impossible or dangerous (no other lanes in your direction), you must slow down until you have passed the vehicle. The correct slow speeds are listed below. On a four-lane or more-lane highway, you must slow down to 15 mph less than the posted speed limit. On a two-lane highway, you must slow down to 15 mph less than the posted speed limit if it is 25 mph or higher, or 10 mph otherwise. (Note: Although every state in the United States now has its own Move Over Law, some of them require drivers to do different things. Always check the local traffic laws when traveling out of state.)

Question 24 - Signs and Situations

(D) This lane direction sign is a regulatory sign. Vehicles in the left lane must turn left, while vehicles in the right lane may go straight or turn right.

Question 25 - Signs and Situations

(A) A driver turning left at an intersection must first yield to oncoming traffic and crossing pedestrians. Car A must yield to Car B, who has the right-of-way.

Question 26 - Signs and Situations
(D) In a marked or unmarked crosswalk, a vehicle must yield to pedestrians. In addition, at an uncontrolled intersection (one without signs or signals), each vehicle must yield to the vehicle to its right. As a result, Car A must yield to Car B, who in turn must yield to Car C, who in turn must yield to the pedestrian.

Question 27 - Signs and Situations
(D) This is a yield symbol. Slow down as you approach a yield sign and prepare to yield to pedestrians and traffic ahead. You may need to stop as well, so be prepared.

Question 28 - Signs and Situations
(D) No-Zones are large blind spots on large trucks and buses. In a No-Zone, a car may be completely hidden from the truck driver's view. The truck's side mirrors only provide small arcs of visibility down the sides. A vehicle directly behind or to the side of the truck, just behind the cab, may be in a No-Zone. Car B is currently in one of the truck's No-Zones. It is impossible to always avoid a truck's No-Zones, but don't stay in them for any longer than necessary. Remember that if you can't see the truck driver directly or through one of the truck's mirrors, the truck driver can't see you.

Question 29 - Signs and Situations

(A) Vehicles turning left at an intersection must first yield to oncoming traffic and crossing pedestrians. Car A must yield in this situation.

Question 30 - Signs and Situations
(C) You are not permitted to park within 50 feet of a railroad crossing's nearest rail. (There are numerous other places where you are not permitted to park.) Look for any signs or pavement markings that prohibit or limit parking.

Question 31 - Signs and Situations
(D) When a vehicle hits standing water at a high enough speed, its tires skip across the water's surface, this is referred to as hydroplaning. Because the tires will not be in contact with the road, traction will be minimal. At speeds as low as 35 mph, a vehicle can begin to hydroplane. At 55 mph, the tires may lose contact with the road entirely. A slight turn or even a gust of wind at this point could send the vehicle into an uncontrollable skid. Make sure your tires have enough tread to help prevent hydroplaning. If you come across

Question 32 - Signs and Situations
(D) Hand signals can be used in place of your vehicle's traditional lighted turn and brake signals. This driver intends to make a left turn.

Question 33 - Signs and Situations
(C) You must halt between 15 and 50 feet from the nearest rail when the railroad crossing signals and gates

warn of an approaching train. Use caution and keep an eye on the signals, gates and tracks even after the train has passed, as a second train may arrive soon after the first one. Only until the signals have ceased and the gates have been fully raised may you proceed to cross the tracks.

Question 34 - Signs and Situations
(A) This sign indicates that the maximum speed limit is 50 miles per hour. That is, you are not permitted to exceed 50 mph in this area. Additional signage may be posted to regulate minimum or nighttime speed limits.

Question 35 - Signs and Situations
(C) This sign warns drivers that the road ahead will be divided into a divided highway. A physical barrier, such as a median, will be used to separate opposing lanes. Continue to the right.

Question 36 - Signs and Situations
(B) Unless there is a sign prohibiting it, you may turn left on a red light when turning from one one-way street onto another one-way street. Before turning, you must still come to a complete stop and yield to all pedestrians and traffic. Some states have different laws regarding turning left on red. Always check the local traffic laws when traveling out of state.

Question 37 - Signs and Situations
(A) Turning right on a red light is legal, unless signs are prohibiting it.

However, before turning, you must come to a complete stop and yield to pedestrians and traffic.

Question 38 - Signs and Situations
(A) If you're parking on a hill without a curb, point your front wheels toward the road's edge (i.e., away from traffic). If your brakes fail, your car will roll toward the road's edge rather than into traffic. Make certain that your parking brake is still engaged and that your vehicle is in the proper gear. Shift into park, if you have an automatic transmission. When facing downhill, shift into reverse and when facing uphill, shift into first gear for maximum forward torque.

Question 39 - Signs and Situations
(C) Unless signs or pavement markings indicate otherwise, you should cross as few lanes as possible when turning. That is, you should turn left from the left lane and right from the right lane and then into the nearest lane of traffic moving in the right direction. Car A has correctly turned into the closest lane and then merged into the far lane. Car B has made an incorrect turn into the farthest lane.

Question 40 - Signs and Situations
(B) A flashing red signal must be treated as a stop sign. That is, before entering the intersection, you must stop, yield to traffic and pedestrians and then proceed when it is safe to do so.

Question 41 - Signs and Situations

(B) After yielding to all pedestrians and vehicles already in the intersection, you can proceed on a green signal.

Question 42 - Signs and Situations
(C) This sign indicates the presence of a fire station nearby. Keep an eye out for fire trucks as they enter this road.

Question 43 - Signs and Situations
(B) When you have a green signal, you can proceed after yielding to all oncoming traffic and pedestrians in the intersection. Car A should yield to Car B in this situation.

Question 44 - Signs and Situations
(C) If an emergency vehicle with flashing red or blue lights and a siren approaches from either direction, you must proceed through an intersection, pull over to the curb or side of the road and come to a complete stop.

Question 45 - Signs and Situations
(D) This is an advisory sign advising drivers not to exceed 35 mph in this area.

Question 46 - Signs and Situations
(A) You must yield to oncoming traffic before turning left into an alley or driveway. And, whenever you drive into or out of a driveway or alley, you must come to a complete stop before crossing the sidewalk and yield to pedestrians

Question 47 - Signs and Situations

(B) When parallel parking facing uphill, turn your wheels away from the curb and then roll back slightly so that the back part of the curbside front wheel rests against the curb. The curb will prevent your car from rolling backward if your brakes fail. Make certain that your parking brake is still engaged and that your vehicle is in the proper gear (Park for an automatic transmission or first gear for maximum forward torque, with a manual transmission).

Question 48 - Signs and Situations
(B) When you are within 500 feet of an oncoming vehicle or within 200 feet of a vehicle you are following, you must dim your high beams. Avoid shining your high beams on any other vehicle that is occupied. If you dim your high beams before they shine on other vehicles, those other drivers may reciprocate.

Question 49 - Signs and Situations
(A) When you come to a complete stop at a stop sign, you must do so before the stop line, crosswalk or intersection, whichever comes first. After that, yield to pedestrians and other vehicles and proceed only when the intersection is clear.

Question 50 - Signs and Situations
(D) You must always obey a police officer or a firefighter's instructions, even if it means disregarding other traffic devices or rules. For example, if a police officer waves you through a red light or a stop sign, you should proceed.

FINE & LIMITS

Question 1 - Fines & Limits

(C) The drunk driver is the most likely to be killed in a car accident caused by drunk driving. [Alcohol and Driving, Minnesota Driver's Manual, Chapter 8 Driving Under the Influence of Alcohol or Drugs]

Question 2 - Fines & Limits

(C) If a Minnesota driver under the age of 21 is found to have any measurable level of alcohol in his or her system while driving, his or her license will be suspended for 30 days. [Underage Drinking - No Tolerance Rule, Penalties, Minnesota Driver's Manual, Chapter 8 Driving Under the Influence of Alcohol or Drugs]

Question 3 - Fines & Limits

(C) If you are convicted of driving an uninsured vehicle, you might face a $1,000 fine and up to 90 days in jail. [Insurance, Minnesota Driver's Manual, Chapter 3 Traffic Laws and Vehicle Operation]

Question 4 - Fines & Limits

(B) A first DWI violation is punishable by 90 days in prison and/or a $1,000 fine. [First Offense, Penalties, Chapter 8 of the Minnesota Driver's Manual, Driving Under the Influence of Alcohol or Drugs]

Question 5 - Fines & Limits

(D) No work permit will be provided for your first DWI conviction until a 15-day revocation period has ended and you have satisfied all reinstatement conditions. However, if your blood alcohol content (BAC) was 0.16 percent or more, you will be ineligible for a work permit. (An average 180-pound guy can achieve a BAC of 0.17 percent by taking five shots of 80-proof whiskey, five 12-ounce cans of beer, or 25 ounces of wine before his body begins to break down the alcohol.) [First Offense, Penalties, Chapter 8 of the Minnesota Driver's Manual, Driving Under the Influence of Alcohol or Drugs]

Question 6 - Fines & Limits

(B) A fourth DWI conviction within ten years is considered a crime. A felony DWI can result in a four-year loss of driving privileges, as well as up to seven years in prison and/or a $14,000 fine. [Felony DWI, Penalties, Minnesota Driver's Manual, Chapter 8 Driving Under the Influence of Alcohol or Drugs]

Question 7 - Fines & Limits

(B) Your Minnesota driver's license will be revoked if you commit an offense in another state that would have resulted in license revocation in Minnesota. [Revocation, License Withdrawal, Minnesota Driver's Manual, Chapter 7 Your Driving Privileges]

Question 8 - Fines & Limits

(D) A Minnesota driver's license may be suspended for multiple traffic violations, possession of a forged license, failure to pay a traffic fine when required, and a variety of other offenses. [Suspension, License Withdrawal, Minnesota Driver's Manual, Chapter 7 Your Driving Privileges]

Question 9 - Fines & Limits

(C) If you are convicted of exceeding 100 mph while driving, your driver's license will be suspended for at least six months. [Minnesota Driver's Manual, Chapter 3 Traffic Laws and Vehicle Operation, Speed Limits and Fines]

Question 10 - Fines & Limits

(D) Driving under the influence of drugs is just as dangerous as driving under the influence of alcohol. Driving while under the influence of restricted or dangerous substances is illegal in Minnesota. Illegal and prescribed medications, as well as home goods, are examples of these substances. These substances have the potential to impair a driver's mental and physical abilities to operate a vehicle safely and respond to driving situations. Furthermore, even legal medications that do not cause impairment on their own can create potent intoxication effects when combined with alcohol. [Drugs and Driving, Minnesota Driver's Manual, Chapter 8 Driving While Under the Influence of Alcohol or Drugs]

DISTRACTED DRIVING

Question 1 - Distracted Driving

(D) You should also be cautious of the following potential distractions and impairments: 1) Alcohol, narcotics and even some prescriptions can impair your ability to drive. 2) Listening to overly loud music or utilizing technologies such as cell phones, GPS and intercoms while driving can also impair your concentration. 3) Adjusting your vehicle's technological controls and features can be distracting and quickly impair your ability to scan for and react to risks. 4) Emotional and physical states such as exhaustion, rage, illness, worry and terror can all impact your driving abilities.

Question 2 - Distracted Driving

(D) When you are driving, read the label before taking a drug to see if there are any precautions about its side effects. If you are unsure if it is safe to take the medication and drive, consult your doctor or pharmacist about any potential adverse effects. Drugs used to treat headaches, colds, hay fever or other allergies or to calm nerves might make a person drowsy and impair driving ability. Other prescription medicines ingredient, like alcohol, can impair your reflexes, judgment, eyesight and awareness.

Question 3 - Distracted Driving

(B) Turning around to attend to the needs of passengers, children or pets should not distract your attention away from the road. If you need to tend to passengers or animals, pull over to the side of the road and park.

Question 4 - Distracted Driving

(B) Before you begin your journey, you should customize your cab to your liking, however eating and drinking should be done at rest stops.

Question 5 - Distracted Driving

(D) Stimulants, exercise and music can help you stay awake, but the greatest solution for drowsiness is sleep. Consult a doctor if you're getting 9 hours of sleep but still feeling fatigued.

Question 6 - Distracted Driving

(D) The monotony of the road and traffic, the buzz of the wind, tires and engine noise all contribute to highway hypnosis or dizziness when driving. Drivers can avoid highway hypnosis by shifting their eyes regularly and paying attention to the traffic and highway signs around them.

Question 7 - Distracted Driving

(A) Driving while using a visual screen device or texting is illegal. Acting in this manner while driving is against the law.

Question 8 - Distracted Driving

(C) Cell phones are not permitted to be used by underage drivers while driving unless to notify an emergency.

Question 9 - Distracted Driving

(B) Even on a straightaway or an empty road, a distraction is still a distraction. While driving, do not eat, drink, smoke, text, read or engage in unpleasant conversations. If at all feasible, turn off your phone and leave it turned off until you are finished driving for the day.

Question 10 - Distracted Driving

(D) Texting or eating while driving raises your chances of being involved in an accident. If you get lost, pull over and enter navigation directions. You can, however, utilize audio navigation while driving.

Question 11 - Distracted Driving

(D) Many prescription and over-the-counter drugs have the potential to make you drowsy. Take drugs while driving only if your doctor says they won't impair your ability to drive safely.

Question 12 - Distracted Driving

(D) Talking on a cell phone while driving increases your chances of being in a crash by up to four times. This is because the talk is diverting your focus away from your driving. Sending text messages (texting) while driving increases your chances of getting involved in an accident by up to eight times.

Question 13 - Distracted Driving

(A) Any activity that takes your eyes off the road while driving, such as removing clothing, doing makeup, reading, eating or drinking, is risky.

Do not carry someone, a pet or a package in your lap or arms.

Question 14 - Distracted Driving

(A) Anything that takes your attention away from the road can cause you to become distracted. Texting, talking on the phone, dealing with children and lighting a cigarette are all examples of distractions while driving.

Question 15 - Distracted Driving

(A) Texting and driving is currently the biggest cause of death among teenagers, accounting for 25% of all car accidents in the United States. It is against the law to send text texts while driving.

Question 16 - Distracted Driving

(D) Prescription drugs, illegal narcotics and over-the-counter medications can all impair your ability to drive safely.

Question 17 - Distracted Driving

(B) If you are an adult driver and really must use your phone while driving, utilize a speakerphone/hands-free device. Using a cell phone while driving is not encouraged and is even illegal in some places.

Question 18 - Distracted Driving

(C) It is illegal for a minor to drive while using a cell phone. If his or her cell phone rings, he or she should not answer it. Violations of this law are punishable by fines.

Question 19 - Distracted Driving

(D) Fatigue can impair your judgment, lower your reaction times and reduce your awareness of your surroundings when driving.

Question 20 - Distracted Driving

(A) Any activity that requires you to use your hands while driving should be avoided. Listening to the radio, on the other hand, can assist you in remaining alert.

DRINKING AND DRIVING

Question 1 - Drinking and Driving
(D) It is illegal for a minor between the ages of fifteen and twenty-one to be in the possession of alcohol, consume alcohol, attempt to purchase or purchase alcohol, or have a blood alcohol concentration (BAC) of 0.02 percent or higher.

Question 2 - Drinking and Driving
(D) All of the responses have the same quantity of alcohol.

Question 3 - Drinking and Driving
(A) The presence of open containers of alcohol in any area within reach of the vehicle's driver or passenger is prohibited by the Open Container Law. Limousines, taxis, motor homes and commercial buses are exempt.

Question 4 - Drinking and Driving
(D) Alcohol can impair your concentration, reaction time and decision-making abilities.

Question 5 - Drinking and Driving
(A) According to the National Safety Council, someone dies in an alcohol-related crash every 33 minutes. Drunk driving is the leading single cause of death in young people aged 16 to 24. According to statistics, 112 million US drivers drank too much and went behind the wheel in 2010.

Question 6 - Drinking and Driving
(D) Your blood alcohol content is affected by how quickly you drink, how many drinks you've had and how much you weigh (BAC).

Question 7 - Drinking and Driving
(D) Regardless of the form, one drink typically contains a one and a half ounce serving of alcohol.

Question 8 - Drinking and Driving
(B) Drinking alcohol and driving at night is extremely risky because your vision is already limited due to the darkness and difficulty of seeing.

Question 9 - Drinking and Driving
(D) A drunk driver is more prone to drive too fast or too slowly, to change lanes repeatedly and to fail to dim the headlights. Even more importantly, in an emergency, an intoxicated driver may be less aware and may take too long to brake. Such errors may jeopardize both the driver and others.

Question 10 - Drinking and Driving
(D) When you consume alcohol, it enters your system and begins to influence all of your bodily processes, including coordination, self-control and reaction time. The only 'cure' for alcohol's effects on the brain is to wait for it to leave your system.

Question 11 - Drinking and Driving
(A) Only time can clear alcohol from one's system. People wrongly believe that coffee and fresh air will conceal the effects of alcohol, such

as tiredness and slowed reactions, but they will not change the fact that you will be driving under the influence until a sufficient amount of time has passed after drinking.

Question 12 - Drinking and Driving
(A) By operating a motor vehicle, you have consented to submit to a chemical test if asked by a police officer if you are arrested for driving under the influence of intoxicants.

Question 13 - Drinking and Driving
(D) Open containers of alcohol may only be stored in areas where drivers and passengers cannot reach them, such as cargo areas, trunks and truck beds.

Question 14 - Drinking and Driving
(D) Alcohol can impair vision, slow reaction times and dull judgment. Alcohol has no effect on alertness.

Question 15 - Drinking and Driving
(D) Alcohol use before or while driving impairs reflexes, physical control of a vehicle and awareness of potential hazards on the road.

Question 16 - Drinking and Driving
(D) If you intend to drink alcohol, you should also plan to use public transportation, a taxi or arrange a designated driver to go home.

Question 17 - Drinking and Driving
(D) If you are convicted of driving under the influence of alcohol or drugs, you could face license suspension, steep fines and community service.

Question 18 - Drinking and Driving
(D) Unless you are 21 years old, you are not permitted to purchase, drink or possess alcohol.

Question 19 - Drinking and Driving
(B) The amount of alcohol that each person can consume before exceeding the legal limit varies from person to person and is determined by a number of factors.

Question 20 - Drinking and Driving
(D) Even a modest amount of alcohol can impair a driver's reflexes, driving ability and depth perception.

Question 21 - Drinking and Driving
(B) The type of alcohol has no effect on the blood alcohol content. Each type of alcohol has the same amount in a standard serving.

Question 22 - Drinking and Driving
(D) Your driver's license will be suspended if you are a juvenile and are convicted of driving under the influence of drugs or transporting an open container of any alcoholic beverage.

Question 23 - Drinking and Driving
(C) The more alcohol that enters your body to intoxicate you, the longer it will take your liver to break it down. One normal drink (one ounce of hard liquor, one-half glass of wine or a 12-ounce can of beer) can be broken down by the liver in roughly an hour. If you drink a lot of

alcohol, it can take up to a day or two for your body to fully recover.

Question 24 - Drinking and Driving
(A) To drive your vehicle, you must nominate a designated driver. The designated driver is in charge of transporting friends or family members, who have consumed alcoholic beverages, safely.

Question 25 - Drinking and Driving
(A) If you refuse to submit to the requisite blood and/or urine test(s), your driving privileges may be revoked.

EXAM TEST PRACTICE

Question 1 - Mock Exam

(B) You should signal for at least 100 feet before making a turn.

Question 2 - Mock Exam

(D) Use your low-beam headlights and fog lights when driving in fog. However, if fog totally closes in and visibility is reduced to near zero, pull as far off the road as possible and come to a complete stop. Before going, wait for visibility to improve.

Question 3 - Mock Exam

(B) You are not permitted to turn in the direction of the red arrow. Before you can turn, you must first wait for the signal to change to a green arrow or green light.

Question 4 - Mock Exam

(D) The large blind spaces around a commercial vehicle, such as a truck, are referred to as "no zones." These blind zones can be large enough to entirely conceal your vehicle from the commercial vehicle's driver.

Question 5 - Mock Exam

(C) When a vehicle is parallel parked properly next to a curb, its wheels on the curb side should be no more than 12 inches from the curb.

Question 6 - Mock Exam

(A) When a school bus comes to a complete stop with its red lights flashing and its stop arm extended, you must stop at least 20 feet away, regardless of which direction the bus is heading.

Question 7 - Mock Exam

(D) If another vehicle unexpectedly cuts in front of you, don't use the brakes hard without first checking the traffic behind you. If you quickly and unexpectedly slow down, you may be rear-ended by a car directly behind you. Instead, remove your foot off the gas and let your vehicle slow down on its own.

Question 8 - Mock Exam

(D) A double solid yellow line separates opposing traffic lanes and makes passing on both sides of the line illegal.

Question 9 - Mock Exam

(C) Parking within 10 feet of a fire hydrant is illegal in Minnesota. (Note: Other states have different minimum distances.) Always verify the local traffic laws when going out of state.)

Question 10 - Mock Exam

(D) You may not send text messages while driving if you are using a hand-held cell phone, according to the Minnesota Driver's Manual. Adult drivers are also prohibited from using a hand-held cell phone while driving as of August 1, 2019.

Question 11 - Mock Exam

(A) A center turn lane may only be used to make a left turn; it may never be used to pass another vehicle.

Question 12 - Mock Exam

(D) Before changing lanes, check your mirrors and then look over your shoulder to check for blind spots.

Question 13 - Mock Exam

(C) Before passing a bicyclist heading in your direction, make sure the bicyclist is not making or signaling a left turn. When passing a bicycle, Minnesota law requires that you provide at least three feet of space between the side of your vehicle and the bicycle. If you have this much clearance, you can cross the centerline of the road if you are not in a no-passing zone.

Question 14 - Mock Exam

(D) In a marked or unmarked crosswalk, you must always yield to a pedestrian.

Question 15 - Mock Exam

(A) Before going into the passing lane, always activate your turn signal.

Question 16 - Mock Exam

(C) A lane with a diamond symbol is designated for specific types of vehicles. High-occupancy vehicle (HOV) lanes, bus lanes, and cycling lanes are a few examples. Traffic signs will identify which cars are permitted to use the lane.

Question 17 - Mock Exam

(B) If you need to switch lanes, do so one at a time to lessen the likelihood of an accident. Other drivers may not be paying attention to risks in many lanes.

Question 18 - Mock Exam

(A) Driving at fast speeds on wet roads can be dangerous because your tires can lose contact with the road (hydroplane).

Question 19 - Mock Exam

(B) To notify that a train is approaching or passing, several signals (flashing lights, bells, or gates) are used. It is never permissible to ignore these indications and cross nevertheless.

Question 20 - Mock Exam

(D) High beams in front of a vehicle can be blinding; high beams behind a motorist can be distracting. When you're within 1,000 feet of an oncoming vehicle or 200 feet of a vehicle you're following, turn your headlights to low beam.

Question 21 - Mock Exam

(C) Keep your wheels straight when waiting to make a left turn at an intersection. If you mistakenly rear-end another vehicle while pointing your front wheels to the left, you may be pushed into the path of an oncoming vehicle.

Question 22 - Mock Exam

(D) Carbon monoxide is a poisonous, odorless, and colorless gas emitted by engines. It can accumulate inside your vehicle when the windows are closed, or in your garage if your motor is idling. The first signs of carbon monoxide poisoning include lethargy, headache, dizziness, and nausea. If you see any of these signs, immediately open the windows, turn off the engine, and exit the car or garage. The only way to recover from carbon monoxide poisoning is to get enough fresh air.

Question 23 - Mock Exam

(D) Bicycles are legal vehicles in Minnesota, and bicyclists have the same rights and obligations as drivers of other vehicles. At an uncontrolled intersection (one without signs or signals), the vehicle that arrives first, whether a vehicle or a bicycle, has the right-of-way.

Question 24 - Mock Exam

(B) When turning left from a one-way street onto a two-way street, begin in the left lane.

Question 25 - Mock Exam

(B) When you can't see more than 500 feet ahead, you must use your headlights. In inclement weather, you must also use your headlights.

Question 26 - Mock Exam

(C) Lower posted speed restrictions are common in work zones. If there is no posted speed limit, you may travel no faster than 45 mph if workers are present.

Question 27 - Mock Exam

(C) If the brakes on a vehicle facing downhill fail, it may roll forward. As a result, when parking your vehicle facing downhill, you should take the following precautions to prevent it from rolling away: Turn your front wheels in the direction of the curb. Shift into Park (for an automatic transmission) or Reverse (for a manual transmission) (for a manual transmission). Apply the parking brake.

Question 28 - Mock Exam

(A) Lanes of traffic driving in the same direction are separated by broken or solid white lines.

Question 29 - Mock Exam

(A) Unless there are signs or signals indicating otherwise, you should begin and finish a right turn in the right lane.

Question 30 - Mock Exam

(C) If a vehicle approaches from the left with its turn signal on while you are waiting at a stop sign to turn right, you should wait until the other vehicle has actually begun to turn. Then and only then should you begin your turn. Drivers are prone to making mistakes or changing their minds.

Question 31 - Mock Exam

(C) A double solid white line separates two lanes of traffic driving in the same direction, yet it is illegal to cross a double solid white line. On freeways, double solid white lines are commonly used to separate a high-occupancy vehicle (HOV) lane from other lanes driving in the same direction.

Question 32 - Mock Exam

(B) If you see a yield sign, it means you should slow down and prepare to stop if a vehicle or pedestrian is approaching from the opposite way. When approaching a yield sign, a vehicle driving from the opposite direction with the right-of-way should not have to brake to prevent colliding with you.

Question 33 - Mock Exam

(B) If your car collides with a parked vehicle or other property, leave a note with your name, address, and phone number and secure it to the vehicle or property you hit. Notify the police and file all necessary accident reports.

Question 34 - Mock Exam

(C) You must always yield to pedestrians the right-of-way.

Question 35 - Mock Exam

(A) Hills and curves on rural roads are frequently higher and sharper than on highways. Before reaching the crest of a hill or entering a curve, slow down, move to the right side of the road, and watch for oncoming vehicles.

Question 36 - Mock Exam

(C) When traveling in wide terrain with no traffic in sight, you should use high beams. High lights allow you to see further ahead, but they can also blind the driver of another car. They can also reflect precipitation, resulting in glare. When traveling behind another car or when another vehicle is coming, use low beams. In addition, use low beams when there is fog, rain, or snow.

Question 37 - Mock Exam

(D) The brakes may fade if you continue to apply them to manage your speed on a steep slope (lose their effectiveness). Instead, let go of the gas and move into a lower gear (even with an automatic transmission). This will produce a braking effect, known as engine braking, to slow the car. The stronger the engine braking impact, the lower the gear. Only use the brakes when engine braking is insufficient or you wish to come to a complete stop.

Question 38 - Mock Exam

(D) Steer right toward the shoulder or curb to prevent a head-on collision. Do not veer left; the other car may attempt to re-enter the proper lane. To escape a head-on accident, be prepared to drive completely off the road to the right. Accidents involving a head-on collision are frequently fatal.

Question 39 - Mock Exam

(C) Vehicles coming from either direction may make a left turn in the central lane.

Question 40 - Mock Exam

(C) If you are in a junction and an emergency vehicle approaches you with a siren, an air horn, or a red or blue flashing light, you must clear the intersection and move over to the right to allow the emergency vehicle to pass. A roundabout is one example of an intersection. If you're at a roundabout, keep going until you reach your exit, then pull over to the right and let the emergency vehicle pass.

A MESSAGE FROM THE DRIVING SCHOOL

First and foremost, we want to thank you for choosing this book. We hope it has, in some manner, added value to your life.

If you enjoyed this book and found the practice tests useful, please let us know. We would greatly appreciate it, if you could leave a review on Amazon.

Your feedback and support will be invaluable in assisting us, to improve our next books and make the current one even better.

Thank you so much,

The Driving School

Made in the USA
Monee, IL
03 September 2024

65102492R00125